Celebrating, Honoring, and Valuing Rich Traditions

The History of the Ohio Appalachian Arts Program

WRITTEN FOR THE OHIO ARTS COUNCIL

By

Wayne Rapp

Lucky Press

Published by
Lucky Press, LLC
126 South Maple Street
Lancaster, Ohio 43130
www.luckypress.com

ISBN-10: 0-9776300-3-X   ISBN-13: 978-0-9776300-3-5

PRINTED IN THE UNITED STATES OF AMERICA

Cover Illustration by Angel McIlwain
Book Design by Janice Marie Phelps

Library of Congress Cataloging-in-Publication Data

Rapp, Wayne, 1939-
Celebrating, honoring, valuing, rich traditions : the history of the
Ohio Appalachian Arts Program / written for the Ohio Arts Council
by Wayne Rapp.
p. cm.
ISBN-13: 978-0-9776300-3-5 (pbk. : alk. paper)
ISBN-10: 0-9776300-3-X (pbk. : alk. paper)
1. Government aid to the arts--Ohio. 2. Government aid to the arts--
Appalachian Region. 3. Ohio Appalachian Arts Program. I. Ohio Arts
Council. II. Title.
NX742.O32A677 2006
700.79'771--dc22
2006003213

The Ohio Arts Council is a state agency that funds and supports quality arts experiences to strengthen Ohio communities culturally,
educationally and economically. Visit www.ArtsinOhio.com to learn
about arts and cultural events within Ohio.

Information on purchasing additional copies of *Celebrating, Honoring,
and Valuing Rich Traditions: The History of the Ohio Appalachian Arts
Program* can be found online at www.luckypress.com/appalachia.
Group, business, library, and association discounts are available by
contacting the publisher at 740-689-2950. This book is also available at
Amazon.com and fine booksellers everywhere.

*Dedicated to Wayne P. Lawson
whose vision of inclusion shone a light
on the Arts in Appalachian Ohio.*

Table of Contents

Foreword

In the first few minutes after I met Donna Sue Groves for the first time, she began to tell a story about an elderly man in adult day-care in Portsmouth, Ohio. He would show up at the day-care site each day angry, withdrawn, frustrated, and he would spend his day that way. Things changed when the center received a grant from the Ohio Arts Council to bring local musicians into the facility to play for the residents and to interact with them. The man, a former musician, began to respond to the music. By the end of the year, he was sitting up straight in his wheelchair; he was primping and combing his hair and telling his children about what was happening. He was also engaging and testing the musicians, trying to trick them. Asking them if they knew who wrote what song. When the man died, the family asked one of the musicians to do the eulogy at his funeral service. The musical experience had value for the man, his family, and the musicians.

I was to hear stories like this one as I traveled through Appalachian Ohio and West Virginia during the following weeks. I learned very quickly that the arts can change lives, can lift burdens, can make a meager, difficult existence more bearable. For this experience, the seeds of which were sown during the very first conversation I had about Appalachian arts, I am most grateful.

1

Abandoned

Sometimes his mind flew black as a crow
Over hundreds of coves and hollers
Fallen silent since the people were swept
Out like rafted logs on spring's high water

Then his life would stand
Empty as an abandoned house
In one of those forgotten places,
His days like blackened chimneys
Standing in fields going back
To thickets of second growth—
Untended tombstones in a cemetery
Up some lost valley.

Sometimes he thought there was nothing left
But the life of a half-wild dog
And the shelter of a junked car
Turned on its back in a ditch, half
Grown over with honeysuckle.

Or else his life became the house
Seen once in a coalcamp in Tennessee:
The second story blown off in a storm
So stairs led up into the air
and stopped.

–Jim Wayne Miller

J im Wayne Miller is often called the Poet Laureate of Appalachia. Abandoned houses, forgotten places, untended tombstones, junked cars. The imagery he uses in his poetry mirrors the plight of Appalachians: abandoned, run off, cut off, often living somewhere else but never forgetting roots, forever looking toward home in the hills, across the ridges, or in the valleys along the river.

When Miller selected images for the last lines of this mournful poem, he might also have been describing the condition of Appalachian arts in Ohio: a stairway extending upward into the middle of nowhere, its future unconnected. Only nobody knew that yet. The work had not yet been done. Later — after the surveys, and the meetings, and the face-to-face encounters with artists, sculptors, musicians, quilters, writers, and the other gifted and creative craftspeople in twenty-nine counties — the Ohio Arts Council team could see that Miller described what they had discovered during all the late nights and many miles of travel: the arts in Appalachian Ohio had a strong base, one that had managed to withstand neglect, indifference, and disappointment. But its creators were often unconnected — to each other and to the various arts organizations in the region — like the steps that led up into the air and stopped.

The goal of the Ohio Arts Council then was to become a building partner with the Appalachian artists, providing funding to buy some of the materials, to pay for an architect (advisor) when they could, to guide artists through the maze of permits and variances (paperwork). And, when necessary, to work shoulder-to-shoulder with arts organizations and individual artists, doing the physical labor necessary to push the building upward, to connect the open steps to a second floor, and a third if necessary, until the structure (a program of Appalachian Arts) was complete and stood as a symbol of hope in the region, one that made people proud and helped celebrate their Appalachian heritage. This is the story of that effort: the vision carried out by dedicated people, the successes and disappointments, and the continuing work that is the Ohio Appalachian Arts Program.

"To create one's own world,
in any of the arts, takes courage."

Georgia O'Keeffe, Painter

2

A Word from the Appalachees

In the beginning was that strange-sounding word: Appalachian. Hernando de Soto named the long mountain range that stood in the way of his voyage of discovery after the Appalachee tribe of Muskhogean Indians he encountered in Florida and Georgia. He mistakenly thought the tribe lived in those mountains. Years later, Americans would learn to identify Appalachia as a region in the Eastern and Southeastern parts of the country that generally follows the landscape of a series of long ridges divided into several ranges of mountains. People living in that region appropriately are referred to as Appalachians.

Map of Appalachia. (Appalachian Regional Commission)

In 1965, as part of Lyndon Johnson's War on Poverty, the Appalachian Regional Development Act (ARDA) was passed with the bipartisan support of Congress. The act established an Appalachian Regional Commission (ARC) and defined Appalachia in specific geographical terms. It established boundaries for an area of 200,000 square miles that traversed the spine of the Appalachian Mountains from southern New York State to northern Mississippi. Included in the region were over 23 million people in 410 counties across thirteen states.

The boundaries were surprising to some. Prior to this specific geographic definition of the region, few people might have thought of Appalachia as including states such as New York, Maryland, or Pennsylvania. The term had always had a more southern connotation. In Ohio, twenty-eight counties were part of the original designation. They basically formed the southern and eastern boundaries of the state. Columbiana County joined the list in 1989, becoming eligible for commission money.

Geography aside, the overriding characteristic of counties identified as being part of the Appalachian region was poverty. Statistics showed that one in three Appalachians lived in poverty with a per capita income twenty-three percent lower than the U.S. average. High unemployment in the region during the 1950s had forced more than two million people to leave their homes and seek jobs elsewhere. ARC's goal, then, was to develop programs that would provide economic development in the region, curbing the migration flow and giving the residents an opportunity not only to stay but to lead lives of hope and dignity.

The idea to establish a specific office in the State of Ohio that would be responsible for representing the Appalachian region did not come for more than twenty years after the creation of ARC. In 1986, the state, through passage of House Bill 891, established the Ohio Office of Appalachia, and Governor Richard Celeste appointed the first director. Eventually, the

Governor's Office of Appalachia was created, and all functions relating to the region were consolidated in one office in 1991. Appalachian Ohio now had an organization to support their specific interests in state government.

While the Appalachian Regional Commission and the Governor's Office of Appalachia have been successful in meeting their goals, the region is often miscast in stereotypical terms in other parts of the country. Aren't all Appalachians poor? And aren't all poor people either ignorant or lazy, or both? A drain on the welfare system? Popular culture in general and the entertainment industry in particular continued to stigmatize the Appalachian region with a hillbilly brand that is a source of derision. Where were to be found those strong, warm, sincere characteristics of the real people of Appalachia: self-reliance, pride, family solidarity, neighborliness, sense of humor, and patriotism? Someone needed to answer that question.

3

Beginning to Serve
the Underserved

Establishment of a Minority Arts Program at the Ohio Arts Council was the first step in beginning to serve the underserved, and that idea originated in a personal philosophy of service held by Executive Director, Wayne Lawson. "I'm a great believer in public service," he says. "I was a child of the '60s and very much a believer in Kennedy's speech where he said, 'Ask not what your country can do for you, but what you can do for your country.' Coming from that kind of background, you're more alert to what's going on. I think in my mind, I was anticipating the changes that were taking place: the lack of funding, the lack of support, the lack of involvement, the lack of inclusivity. Where were the people of color? On the staff? On the board? On the panels? Then looking at the grants and thinking, 'We're not funding very many organizations run by or supporting people of color.' "

Wayne Lawson has held the position of executive director of the Ohio Arts Council since 1978. Prior to coming to the agency, he served as the first chairman of the Comparative Literature Department at The Ohio State University. Born in Cleveland, Wayne received a BA in romance languages, an MA in European literature, and a Ph.D. in theater and comparative literature, all from The Ohio State University. Throughout his career in the arts, this highly respected man has been a leader of national and international committees and organizations. His beliefs in aiding the underserved led him to chair the Arts in Underserved Communities Panel of the National Endowment for the Arts' State and Regional Programs. Among his many honors is recognition by the Association of American Cultures for leadership and commitment to the development of cultural diversity in the arts. Wayne Lawson is firm in his commitment that the Ohio Arts Council will provide access to its resources to all the citizens of the state.

Lawson remembers that, for him, it was former Governor Richard Celeste that really kick-started the idea of serving Appalachia by urging government agencies to do something to serve the underserved in the State of Ohio. "And so we started a program. There was no specific plan. We just knew it was the right thing to do."

Those who have worked with Wayne Lawson at the Ohio Arts Council know that his management style is to provide his staff with plenty of freedom to help define the projects he assigns. In this case, the project went to a new hire, Barbara Bayless. "Wayne throws out ideas and lets you run with them." She discovered what other staff members already knew.

During over twenty-five years of service to the people of Ohio through the Ohio Arts Council, Barbara Bayless has done just about everything. She was the first coordinator for the Individual Artist Program, and she has been coordinator for traditional arts and for festivals as well. Her first job, and the reason she was hired at OAC, though, was the beginning of the commitment to serve the underserved in Ohio.

"When Wayne hired me in '78 to start the Minority Arts Program, he determined that in addition to African American, Asian American, Native American, and Latinos, that Appalachia needed to be included in that group," Barbara remembers.

Barbara embraced the idea. She was a young African American with two children who had transferred, along with her husband who was in the military, to Columbus from Springfield, Ohio. In

Columbus, she was able to resume an education she had started at Wittenberg University and abandoned after a year to begin a family. After she graduated from Ohio State with a degree in art education in 1975, she worked as docent coordinator at the Columbus Museum of Art before joining the Ohio Arts Council.

While Barbara was enthusiastic about setting up the Minority Arts Program, there were no guidelines, and she knew she couldn't do it without help — some input from those who the program would serve. She hired two consultants to help her gather the information she needed. Michael London was one of them. He was part of a year-long planning group that determined what the program would be. "I've had a working relationship with the Minority Arts Program since its inception," he says.

Michael brought an unusual minority perspective to the project. His father was part Scots-Irish and Native American, and his mother was full-blooded Italian, a descendent from coal miners brought from Italy to West Virginia. Michael was born in the hills of West Virginia and was well immersed in the culture of Appalachia, especially music. He grew up in Dayton, part of a family that headed back to West Virginia as often as possible on weekends.

His connection to the arts was strong. He studied at The Ohio State University, Columbia Pacific University, and Lamar University, gaining training as a playwright and as a dancer while earning BA and MA degrees. He completed post graduate studies at Sinclair and Wright State Universities. He was managing director of the Dayton Contemporary Dance Company, an African American dance group, and served on the boards of many arts organizations. He was also a member of the faculty at Wright State University in Dayton.

Michael was part of the first Minority Arts Task Force in 1978. That effort led to the creation of the Ohio Arts Council's Minority Arts Program. He returned as a consultant about a year after the program was underway to help provide the groundwork for the establishment of a short-term technical assistance component for the program. He followed it with a long-term assistance component to assure the program would continue to run. A year after Michael came on board — like the good consultant he was — he had worked himself out of a job. The Minority Arts Program was established, and there was a framework to begin serving the underserved of Appalachia.

"The marble not yet carved can hold the form
of every thought the artist has."

Michelangelo Buonarroti,
Painter, Sculptor, Architect

4

Building the Framework

In the mid '80s, another consultant who would have a profound impact on the development of an Appalachian Arts Program came on board for a project. He was Michael Maloney, a Cincinnati resident who, although uncomfortable placing himself in that position, has become an expert in Appalachian culture.

This soft-spoken Kentuckian talks about himself reluctantly. "My entry into the arts was through Appalachian culture. I am considered an expert in Appalachian culture. I studied it; it's my background, and I've been involved in developing programs for and with Appalachia all my adult life, so I'm a culture specialist. Another title I could reasonably give myself is that I'm an arts organizer."

When Barbara Bayless approached Michael Maloney twenty years ago, she met a man who had studied at the University of Kentucky, Xavier University, and the University of North Carolina. He had an undergraduate degree in philosophy and masters degrees in education and community planning. He was teaching philosophy and Appalachian studies at the University of Cincinnati and Chatfield College. He was founding director of the Urban Appalachian Council in Cincinnati, an organization designed to restore pride and Appalachian identity through such actions as education, job training and access to employment, and establishing neighborhood festivals. He was also helping Catholic Social Services set up a field office in Appalachia for the Diocese of Cincinnati. The focal point of his effort was building pride, a consciousness of heritage, and developing homeless shelters, day-care facilities, and emergency assistance programs.

The Ohio Arts Council asked him to use his experience and his resources to help determine what existed in the way of Appalachian arts, artists, and arts agencies and what was needed to support these individuals and organizations. In other words, he was to ask how the Ohio Arts Council could help the various individuals and organizations build on their foundation to create a structure of arts that would be appreciated not only by the residents of Appalachia, but the entire state.

"When OAC began its Minority Arts Program," Maloney recalls, "people like me thought it was a natural outlet from which to build up people's self confidence and self-esteem. When I first met Barbara Bayless, I could tell that her goals were the same: to build up the community through recognition of Appalachian culture."

The core of the Ohio Arts Council's first Appalachian Outreach Program was the development of *The Directory of Appalachian Artists in Ohio*. While collecting material for a directory seemed more legwork than anything, in the case of the artists' directory, the effort included much more. A major problem was helping arts organizations identify and accept the value of traditional arts.

Michael Maloney remembers: "The organizing process itself of collecting the information was a step in building a network among what you might call the Appalachian arts constituency. As I interviewed people I was, to some degree, an apostle of the gospel of Appalachian identity. If I found — say in Portsmouth — an arts program that didn't recognize traditional arts at all, I would, in my gentle way, ask them why."

Another purpose of the directory was to help artists find work, and, in this, it was successful.

Linda Basye used it for this very purpose in Pike County: to identify artists for projects. Like most arts organizers in Appalachian Ohio, Linda wears more than one hat. She is director of the Pike County

Visitors Bureau and, as past president of Ohio's Appalachian Country, Inc., she continues to serve on that board. This group, identified as OAC, Inc., has united Ohio's twenty-nine Appalachian counties for the promotion of travel and tourism.

"I still have the original first printing of the directory of artists for Appalachian Ohio," Linda says. "Now it's online, but before, they had them listed not only alphabetically but by the art form. Then they had associations listed. It was a very useful book. Anytime I needed to put on a trade show and needed artists to participate or demonstrate, it was really helpful for me to open that book. And if I had a type of art that I wanted particularly to show, I could look up the art and then look up the artist. And it gave all their particular information and how to get hold of them and book them. I've used it many times."

Another challenge in collecting data for the directory was in helping artists identify themselves as such, especially those who came from traditional backgrounds. Because their art originated with ancestors and was passed from generation to generation, these practitioners tended to think what they do is either utilitarian or whimsical and shouldn't be taken seriously as art.

Linda Basye has a thought about the same issue: "A lot of people in Appalachia don't realize the value of what they do. They don't see it as valuable at all. During the Bicentennial, I tried to identify quilters and found over eighty quilters in Pike County and know that's not all. Those are artists. Very valuable artists. The traditional arts will be lost if we don't propagate them. To keep them going, we have to let them know how valuable they really are."

With the help of arts advocates like Linda Basye, it was Michael Maloney's job to convince artists of the value of their art and add their names and essential information to his growing list.

Besides the artist directory that came out of the early outreach program, important contacts were made throughout Ohio's Appalachian region that would become invaluable during later phases of the effort. The Ohio Arts Council had established a presence in the counties that defined Appalachia for the state and was poised to carry their outreach to the next step.

"To fulfill a dream, to be allowed to sweat over lonely labor, to be given a chance to create, is the meat and potatoes of life."

Bette Davis, Actress

5

The Power of Three

R eflecting on what was accomplished on the initial outreach efforts, Wayne Lawson tells why the Ohio Arts Council decided it had to continue taking positive steps in the direction of Appalachia: "As we got into it, we realized how underserved the region really was, so we felt it was a great time to put money in some programs there. It was controversial because we were taking money that the larger institutions around the state felt was theirs."

Controversy or not, the die was cast, and in the fall of 1992, Barbara Bayless began putting together the resources for an effort that would eventually become the Ohio Appalachian Arts Initiative (OAAI).

She gathered three consultants to help her establish the effort, the three very best consultants she could find: Michael Maloney, Michael London, and Beverly Warfield.

Michael Maloney knows that his successful effort on the outreach program of the mid '80s is the reason he was tapped to be part of the group. "Barbara knew from that, frankly, that I could deliver. That not only was I an expert on Appalachian culture, but I had the practical organizing skill that this project needed."

Maloney was very much in accord with the idea of an Appalachian Arts Initiative. He felt it was extremely important to the residents of Appalachia. "Because in Ohio, they were just as underserved a population as traditional minorities," he says.

Regarding Michael London, Barbara Bayless provides part of the justification for selecting him: "One reason I put Michael London on the team is he's able to have rapport with anybody. He's never met a stranger. He can build rapport with the most difficult folks.

"So that's what makes him so valuable — working with all those diverse people."

Michael London had been working with Beverly Warfield in Cleveland on an arts initiative for a neighborhood arts center, but the project wasn't moving forward. Barbara Bayless came in to pull the consultants off the project and asked Michael and Beverly if they wanted to transfer their efforts to a new initiative for Appalachian Arts.

As an African American female with an exten-
sive background in non-profit marketing, Beverly
Warfield had a special interest in any program that
served the underserved. Her undergraduate degree
in speech/telecommunications is from Kent State
University, and she has continued to build on her
education and experience through numerous classes
and workshops in a wide variety of business-related
subjects. She had worked with the Ohio Arts Council
since 1985 as an arts advisor.

Based in Cleveland at the time, Beverly was consulting with a number of organizations including, the
Cleveland YWCA, the Cleveland Urban League, the
United Negro College Fund, the Cleveland Minority
Arts Program, and the Columbus Museum of Art. She
had conducted marketing workshops for minority arts
organizations throughout the state and was frequently
serving on arts advisory committees, boards, and program panels.

Barbara Bayless describes Beverly as one of her
very best consultants. "She knew a lot about organizational development, was organized, and I knew she
would be a good match with the Michaels."

Beverly identifies the balance of the consultant
team: "Everybody brought a different kind of
strength. I thought I would be good in terms of the
processing. I'm really good at dotting the i's and
crossing the t's. Michael Maloney was really good in
terms of identifying the organization and the individ-

uals. Michael London — he is very good at networking with people, getting people to work together, and getting people to feel comfortable in sharing their ideas and feelings, so I just thought it would be a very good team to work with."

The initial objective of the group was to find money in the form of grants to help support their effort. Michael Maloney remembers that the first convening of the group of consultants by Barbara Bayless was to apply for a planning grant. "And we called that the Ohio Appalachian Arts Planning Project. The purpose was to reach out to the underserved rural and urban Appalachian population in Ohio. So it was round two of the Ohio Arts Council's Appalachian outreach."

The money needed was received from the National Endowment for the Arts State and Regional Program: Arts in Underserved Communities. Matching funds were made available through the Ohio Arts Council. The one-year planning project (July 1, 1993 – June 30, 1994) was dedicated to setting up and working with a Project Advisory Committee (PAC) and supporting agencies to develop a three-year arts program plan, the Ohio Appalachian Arts Initiative.

The goal during that year of planning was to determine the needs of people who lived and worked in Appalachian Ohio.

Michael Maloney explains how the group started this beginning phase: "Because of the outreach program in the mid '80s, we had a network of contacts. But we didn't just confine contacts to those we knew personally. We took advantage of other Ohio Arts Council representatives as well. First thing we did was determine who we knew, then we started convening those people and consulting them. There were existing arts leaders in the urban and rural areas that we made darn sure to include."

Michael London finishes the thought. "We leaned heavily on two sources: Michael's knowledge and contacts and Barbara's contacts. Barbara developed a list of people in the region who had applied for and received grants or those who she had come in contact with through the Minority Arts Program. From those lists of sources, we put an advisory committee together for this planning process. Then we asked Michael [Maloney] and Beverly about their contacts, anyone else who could provide valuable information and inform the process."

Once the Advisory Committee was in place, it became a matter of convening them and letting the group tell the three consultants what was important in the way of support for the arts in the region. In this way, the consultants were able to determine the primary unmet cultural needs of the Appalachian community. During the planning year, information was gathered during three open meetings (Rio

Grande College, Chatfield College, and Columbus). Members of the committee and interested people living in the area were invited. All three meetings were very well attended. Even heavy snow at Chatfield College didn't prevent a good turnout.

It was somewhere during this first year that a woman who would become a very important person in the Ohio Arts Council's endeavor to build an Appalachian Arts Program joined the Advisory Committee. She was Donna Sue Groves. Donna Sue was a VISTA (Volunteers in Service to America) working under Hope Taft for Ohio Parents for Drug Free Youth in Adams County. She says she went to the Ohio Arts Council in Columbus seeking help in developing an art activity for her group. While there, she met Barbara Bayless and heard about the arts task force meetings that were scheduled in her area of the state. She showed up for that first meeting, asked questions, found out about other meetings through the newspaper, came back again, and just never stopped coming. She was invited to join the Advisory Committee, and from that time on, she has been a tireless worker, one who has been involved with the planning sessions, the Initiative, and every phase of the development of an Appalachian Arts Program. This commitment and experience would eventually bring her to a leadership role in the effort.

During that year of evaluation, residents of Appalachian Ohio showed strong support for the efforts of the Ohio Arts Council and were generous in sharing their observations on the condition of the arts in the region and what they thought was important to building on that base.

For the consultants, especially Michael Maloney who had built his career through service to Appalachia, and Michael London who had been closely involved in minority arts throughout Appalachia, the findings weren't necessarily surprising. They were, however, documented for the first time in a report for the Ohio Arts Council to study and to begin to formulate a plan to meet the needs of artists and arts agencies in Appalachian Ohio.

Woven throughout the findings was the need for a more positive sense of identity for the region and its people. Not only was the condition affecting the ability of communities to retain or attract industry, it was impacting in a harmful way the performance of Appalachian children in school. The arts were seen as a vehicle to reverse this condition. With arts education often lacking in the schools, however, this would be a difficult obstacle to overcome.

The financial reality of the area was another problem. Without affordability, any effort to reach the underserved was jeopardized. While corporate support and organized philanthropy were lacking to aid in this effort, the area was also rich in organizations that were accustomed to doing art programming with limited financial resources. And there was a core of artists committed to preserving its traditional culture.

The consulting group was able to determine that a strong base in the arts existed. They just needed to build on that by working with state agencies, artists, and arts organizations in developing strategies for marketing Appalachian artists. Networking, consultation, and technical assistance — so important to a marketing effort — would be hindered by the distances between communities and county boundaries, and was a problem to be overcome. There was a strong need expressed in updating the *Directory of Appalachian Artists in Ohio*, and a feeling that it would be an important aid in the marketing effort.

Among other needs that the group uncovered was one to develop more material on Appalachian Ohio and its history, culture, and arts traditions. It would be as valuable within the region as outside. The Ohio Appalachian Conference could help in this regard, at least as an interim annual event that would bring artists together with others concerned about regional identity and development.

At the end of the planning year (June 30, 1994), the Ohio Arts Council, its team of consultants, the Advisory Committee, and the supporting agencies had succeeded in developing a three-year program called the Ohio Appalachian Arts Initiative. Funding for the first year was provided by OAC with expectations of grant money from the National Endowment for the Arts to help fund years two and three. The target area for the program was the southern nineteen counties in Appalachian Ohio and the two urban Appalachian communities of Cincinnati and Dayton. Prior to this time, Appalachia had thought by many to have rural boundaries, but the consultants (two of whom were urban dwellers) knew differently. The cities needed to be included in the Initiative as well.

Nineteen Southern Ohio Counties Served by the
Ohio Appalachian Arts Initiative (OAAI)

"Don't ever compromise your work.
You never compromise what's at the heart
of your soul. I feel strongly about it.
There are other ways to make a living."

Nancy Crow, Quilter and Artisan

6

Exiles in the City

Michael Maloney was born and raised in Appalachia and now lives in the city of Cincinnati. He considers himself in exile. "You could make an argument that Appalachian identity has, at least in part, it's origins in urban ghettos. If you live in the mountains, why do you need to be concerned about it? In the cities, we were being pushed around and laughed at, and we knew we needed to find our identity, and part of us, we drifted back to the mountains."

Whether metaphorically or actually, many people of Appalachian heritage have that longing for home.

It's a favorite theme of Appalachian poet, Jim Wayne Miller. His first stanza of the poem "Turn Your Radio On" sets the scene of an Appalachian in exile.

In "Down Home" Miller goes beyond the longing for an Appalachian home and deals with the reality of a decision that may be irrevocable. Home as he knew it is no longer part of his everyday life.

Turn Your Radio On

He couldn't hear his own thoughts in the city that never slept.
Like a voice on a far-off radio station, his thoughts rose
and fell in a storm of static. The city's rush and roar
even poured through his dreams, boiling up like a waterfall.

Asleep or waking, he tried to keep a sense of direction south.
Lying awake in the smoky carbon darkness of northern nights,
facing east, he kept a knowledge, like a book under his pillow,
that the mountains lay to his right, beyond the mills and warehouses.

But sometimes he'd come awake in darkness and find the room
had turned in the slow current of his sleep. He would not rest
again until he'd righted the room, and sleep was drifting
away from the waterfall's roar toward the quietness of mountains.

But he never drifted home before he woke. He felt so stilled
inside, a breathing silence. It was as if his thoughts had been
a friend, a buddy who went everywhere with him. Now he
turned and found that old companion hadn't followed him here.

Down Home

Those sudden weathers, those awkward
encounters! He kept meeting feelings like
old schoolmates, faces whose names he'd
forgot. He came on feelings he could
enter again only as a stranger might
a house he'd once lived in; feelings like
places changed almost beyond recognition: a
once-green pasture field grown up in
pines too thick ever to enter again. Oh,
some of them he picked up as easily as gripping
this ax by its smooth helve, or the handles
of that plow leaning unused a long time
in the toolshed. But what about those
feelings he came on like graves of
childhood pets — a dog, a brindled cat, a bird —
their little bones in hidden graves
marked only in memory? He had to admit it: he
didn't live here any longer. He was
settled in a suburb, north of himself.

Prior to his death several years ago, Jim Wayne Miller and Michael Maloney were friends. "I'd like to think," Maloney says, "that he got part of his ideas for his *Briar Poems* and others when he worked with us. We had him in Cincinnati as a guest speaker from time to time, and he spoke to us at the Ohio Appalachian Conference. The Cincinnati/Southern Ohio network reached out to him, and he was enriched with that experience, and it was reflected in his poetry."

Miller's poems reflect the reality of the Urban Appalachian, but one of the goals of the Ohio Appalachian Arts Initiative was to provide, through the arts, varied opportunities to reconnect to the culture of one's Appalachian heritage.

That potential audience is quite large. Michael Maloney, in an article he wrote entitled, "Appalachian Migration to Southwestern Ohio," provides the numbers: "The Urban Appalachian Council has estimated that by 1975, at least one million first and second generation Urban Appalachians lived in the non-Appalachian sections of Ohio." He went on to say that twenty-eight percent of Hamilton County, of which Cincinnati is the largest city, was either born in Appalachia or had at least one parent born there. That same study also pointed out that one out of five Appalachians was African American.

The numbers are not daunting to Maloney. He seems to want to break situations down to their most simple terms. "Urban Appalachians are rural people living in the cities," he says. "As you get into the second and third and fourth generations, the memories of the mountains still remain. In my family, the memory remains strong through all the generations. Just because they live in the cities doesn't mean they have a different set of values."

Maloney explains that the way Appalachians settled in the city was very much the way immigrant populations — such as Italians — had done earlier. At least this was true for the blue-collar Appalachians. One group followed another and settled in the same neighborhoods, and in this chain migration, people were able to keep their culture intact. It's often when the neighborhoods start changing that the negative images develop.

"A lot of the negative stereotyping comes from various kinds of victim-blaming that occurs in urban areas," Maloney observes. "If my neighborhood is changing — and it may be changing because older folks are retiring and moving out to more manageable housing — and if the people who move in are different, then everything that is going bad about our neighborhood is blamed on the new people. If some of the new people are Appalachians, and some are trashy, they become the stereotype. Then all Appalachians are like them: kids always in trouble, fathers drink, etc. The Appalachian migration followed the same stereotyping that had been applied to other ethnic groups ahead of them. The jokes were revised a bit, and a few new ones added with the same demeaning results. They are isolated in this case not by long distances, but by cultural differences. If you were a school kid from Appalachian Ohio, you learned very quickly that it's not cool to be from that community in the outside world."

Michael Maloney is a firm believer that the Ohio Appalachian Arts Initiative played a big role in beginning the process that would help change the stereotypical images. First, in identifying Appalachian artists and imbuing them with a sense of the true value of their arts and crafts, and, second, helping support their efforts to present material that represents a positive image of the region and celebrates Appalachian culture.

Maloney is hopeful. "There have been some changes. What this is all about is a cultural revitalization, because people didn't feel good about themselves. The Ohio Appalachian Arts Initiative provided a structure we could use to promote Appalachian culture through the arts. A skeleton for the arts existed, and what the Ohio Arts Council did was add some flesh to that."

"The artist is nothing without the gift,
but the gift is nothing without work."

Emile Zola, Novelist

7

Building Bridges across the River

A t the same time the Ohio Appalachian Arts Initiative got underway, another program was beginning to take root that would be an added boost to artists and arts agencies in the Appalachian counties along the Ohio River that separates the state from its neighbor, West Virginia.

The Ohio River itself was the problem and the focus of the new program. Geographically and politically the river divided the two states. In reality, the people living in the Ohio River Valley didn't live their lives that way. They lived on one side and worked or shopped on the other. The river wasn't a boundary; they simply drove across the bridge to the other side and did whatever they needed or wanted to do.

James Wright, Ohio's finest poet, was born in Martins Ferry, Ohio in 1927, a small town bordered on the east by the Ohio River. Even then, the Wright family life was typical of those who lived along the river. His father worked as a die-setter in a glass factory on the other side of the river in Wheeling, West Virginia. Inspired during his years at Kenyon College by John Crowe Ransom, Wright went on to win a Pulitzer Prize and to die much too soon in 1980 when he was just fifty-three. Martins Ferry was a typical mill town of the period, and much of Wright's poetry explores the hardscrabble life of people living in that environment and also the many people he thought were underserved, the homeless poor and the disenfranchised groups, Native Americans and African Americans. The Ohio River had an impact on his poetry, as well. An example is seen in the first two stanzas of the following poem:

The Old WPA Swimming Pool
in Martins Ferry, Ohio

We knew even then the Ohio
River was dying.
Most of the good men who lived along that shore
Wanted to be in love and give good love
To Beautiful Women, who weren't pretty,
And to small children like me who wondered,
What the hell is this?

When people don't have quite enough to eat
In August, and the river,
That is supposed to be some holiness,
Starts dying,

In effect, the Ohio Arts Council, inspired by such Appalachian artists as James Wright, set about building more bridges, those that would connect the arts with an audience on both sides. In total, twenty-one counties in both states would be impacted.

Wayne Lawson remembers that the idea for starting this new program came about during discussions he had with his West Virginia counterpart, Lakin Cook, at a cocktail party. "I think because we liked each other and admired the work we were doing, we began to wonder why we weren't doing anything together. We just started chatting about the counties along the river. 'What do you have on your side? What do we have?' Because it was Lakin, I could cut through all the extraneous stuff about who had the money and who was presently getting the advantages. We just cut through all that and committed ourselves to doing it. I don't want to say it was easy, but the idea germinated and took hold because of the personalities involved."

Lakin Cook is the other half of the personalities involved in the decision. She is Charleston, West Virginia born and University of Alabama educated with a degree in graphic design and art history. She is currently education manager for the Clay Center in Charleston, West Virginia, an organization devoted to the performing arts. At the time she and Wayne Lawson began their discussions, she was director of the West Virginia Commission on the Arts, a position she held for ten years.

"One of the challenges we found in our funding back in the early '90s was along the Ohio River," Lakin says. "The arts institutions on the West Virginia side were doing more for the communities in Ohio, and they were having difficulty getting funding from the Ohio Arts Council, mainly because the OAC was much more sophisticated than we were in terms of the various programs. We had a very basic grant program."

Lakin recalls that about the time of the discussions, some of the money for the underserved was being made available from the federal government, and she and Wayne Lawson both agreed that the nature of boundaries along the Ohio River was artificial and that they should do something about working together on a program that would benefit the arts in both states.

"Wayne and I did a series of meetings on both sides of the river talking to artists and arts groups about their needs. It was 1993, and the planning process took about a year. At the conclusion, we determined that we would each put some money in the pot and come up with some basic guidelines for programs. One of the things we didn't want to see happen is for the larger, established arts organizations to suck us dry. We wanted to foster some new collaborations that really served both sides of the river and involved people on both sides on a more down home and grass roots level."

In 1994, the Ohio River Border Initiative (ORBI), a joint project of the West Virginia Commission on the Arts and the Ohio Arts Council, was up and running with a pilot program for awarding grants. The entire budget of $20,000 was distributed that first year to those with the best cross-river involvement for their projects.

ORBI was able to capitalize on the enthusiasm that the pilot program generated and wrote two proposals to the NEA for a one-year planning program. Bill Howley, who had been one of the four panelists (two from each state) for the pilot program, was hired as a consultant to do research in the area in an effort to determine the needs of artists and arts agencies. Howley had lived in West Virginia for over twenty years, having moved to the state from the Washington, DC area. He specializes in organizational planning and had also done consulting for the West Virginia Commission on the Arts.

Results of the survey he conducted indicated that artists and arts organizations had a strong interest in developing their work across the river, and another grants program was conducted in 1995. According to Howley, the one change that was made during this grants program was that panelists were selected from outside the region so that no conflict of interest would arise with people well acquainted with individual artists and organizations. That arrangement has been part of the grant program's requirements ever since.

After Howley completed his research with art agencies in counties bordering the river, he presented a plan to the Ohio Arts Council and the West Virginia Commission on the Arts in October of 1996 with recommendations for continued implementation of ORBI. The plan was reviewed and accepted. Using funds from both states, Bill Howley was hired at that point as project director.

Wayne Lawson says that the transition from pilot to up-and-running successful program was not without its problems. "It had some rough periods. We kept applying band aids, but ORBI started floating away, and we decided that we could accomplish more in the region with our field reps."

At about that time, Bill Howley came to the rescue. He knew that the major problem centered on the decision to use the French Art Colony as fiscal agent. Due to legislative restrains, West Virginia could not give money directly to grant petitioners in Ohio. They had to give their funding to the Ohio Arts Council, who in turn gave it to the French Art Colony, who finally got it to the ORBI grantees. If funding was distributed in installments, the process had to be repeated. It was a cumbersome setup that required multiple steps to distribute the grants, and it was handcuffing the program.

Howley approached ArtsBridge, an arts service agency based in Parkersburg and serving Wood County, West Virginia and Washington County, Ohio.

This organization had been the original fiscal agent for the first ORBI grants program but felt that extending operations beyond the two counties on a permanent basis would take up considerable staff time to the detriment of their mission. Bill convinced them that with the organizational structure that was in place, with him as project director doing all the administrative work, it would not be difficult to complete the fiscal function. Bill felt this alignment would also demonstrate a real effort by the agencies to keep ORBI in the hands of the people in the region and not in Columbus and Charleston.

Howley had eliminated a cumbersome problem, and the Ohio and West Virginia arts agencies were back in a position to serve arts organizations along the river in an efficient manner. This type of hands-on, direct action toward problem solving fits in with Bill's idea that ORBI should always remain an initiative and not become a program, since its fluid structure allows it to respond to whatever needs doing in the region.

Lakin Cook sums up ORBI this way: " I think the original vision was pretty flexible, pretty open ended. That's what's nice about it. It was non-bureaucratic and we worked to keep it that way. It's sort of like the little engine that could. It just keeps chugging along doing what it's supposed to do. Not in a glamorous way. I don't think that was its intent. I think its intent was to keep things simple and keep that grass roots feeling going. I would hate to see it get swallowed up."

If the program is changed, it won't be by Richard Ressmeyer, Director of Arts for West Virginia. Ressmeyer, who was born and raised in New York City, married a West Virginia woman, and came to the state in the '70s as a curator and educator for a museum. He felt West Virginia could provide very rich cultural advantages to him and his children. He has not been disappointed.

He has been the top arts administrator in the state for five years. Upon coming onboard, he quickly discovered that there were some programs that he didn't need to tinker with. "The Ohio River Border Initiative was running well when I got here, so the credit goes to the people who planned it so many years ago. It was working well, so we didn't feel the need to try to fix it. Too many groups change their original purpose, but ORBI has been true in both scope and scale to its original purpose."

Ressmeyer says that the success of ORBI, the proven idea that two states can transcend their border for the betterment of arts on both sides of the river, has led to discussions of adding another neighbor, Kentucky, to the border mix. It's the natural way to operate along the Ohio River. "In some cases, I think back to the Northwest Territories when the border meant something to somebody, and the legislatures could tax us on one side of the river or the other. But we do commerce together; we have families across the border; we have churches that attract congregations from different sides of the river, and we have artists who consider their neighbors as part of their audience, so that gives it a community character that you don't always have even in one town in a single state."

Besides serving as a clearing house for arts related issues on both sides of the river and providing technical assistance for the business side of arts projects through workshops, ORBI also established and continues to maintain a comprehensive database of individuals and organizations in the arts. The listing is designed to put potential partners, presenters, and performers together for the mutual benefit of the Ohio River Valley.

There is another advantage as well, according to Ressmeyer. "Not everyone who applies to ORBI sees it as a step to larger, bigger, more complicated grants. Some do, and that potential remains, but for some people it becomes the way they relate to public funding."

Bill Howley follows up on the history of the ORBI funding program. He remembers that Ohio and West Virginia drew the boundaries around the counties that tracked the Ohio River and then each put in $10,000 to get the grant program started. *(See facing page.)*

Lakin Cook recalls that one of the things that drew a lot of attention in the beginning of the grant program is that it was an open panel. "That had not happened in West Virginia. Ohio was doing it that

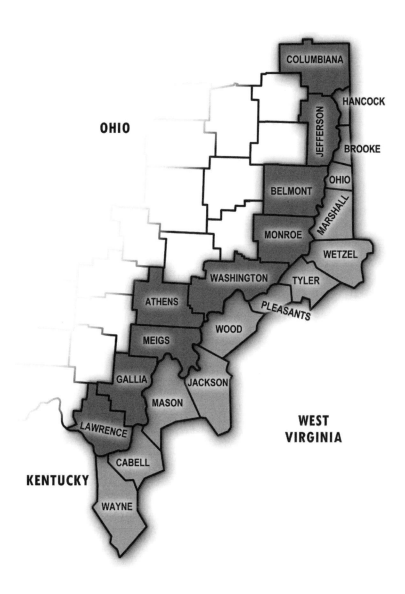

*Ohio and West Virginia Counties Served by
the Ohio River Border Initiative (ORBI)*

way, but we had not. That was unique to us. We also saw it as a learning process for the participants."

The informality of the grant process was also unique. Prior to ORBI, Lakin says that the smaller groups in West Virginia and Ohio were kind of blown away by the bureaucracy of the arts organizations in those states.

ORBI offers two grants opportunities to those individual artists and arts organizations living or operating in the river counties. The Artist Fast Track Grant Program is limited to grants of $500, which are offered to individual artists to fill specific needs, such as personal development in their craft or to purchase materials needed to present their work. The grant cannot be used by individuals to produce their art.

"What we found was that the main ORBI program was not serving the individual artists," Howley says. "So we created an entry-level professional development grant program. People could apply sixty days before they needed the money. There is no matching funds requirement, and the application is relatively simple."

Bill goes on to explain that the Artist Fast Track Grant Program is an innovative collaboration between ORBI and the Ohio Appalachian Arts Program. Both ORBI and OAAP share publicity and use the same application forms. OAAP funds Ohio artists with its own application review process, and ORBI does the same for West Virginia artists.

Members of ORBI's Advisory Committee review West Virginia applications and make final funding decisions. ORBI continues to process Fast Track applications throughout the year until budgeted funding runs out for that year's program.

Bill tells a story about talking to a writer regarding the Fast Track Program in a phone conversation. "She said, 'Now I've never applied for anything like this before, because I don't like taking handouts.' I had to convince her that it was not a handout but an investment in her future."

The writer was Nancy Merical from the small town of Ripley in Jackson County. A native West Virginian, born in Charleston, she writes mostly religious and inspirational stories that promote values from her Appalachian upbringing. Nancy was first published in 1990, but not without help. "I got eighty-four rejections and couldn't understand why. When I finally went to a writers' conference, all of a sudden I understood. I had just been shotgunning everything out. I would send anything to anybody. Didn't know what their guidelines were. I needed that conference to get that kind of information."

Nancy will use her Fast Track grant to go to another conference, this one the St. David Christian Writers' Conference in Pennsylvania. Her goal is to find an agent there. After years of publishing in monthly periodicals, she has found it more difficult to have pieces accepted because of increasing competition in the field. She has turned to self-publishing and has released several books. She feels an agent is the next step in being able to introduce her work to a broader market.

Regarding the ORBI grant, Nancy says, "I could not go to this conference and display or promote my work without it. I think it's very valuable. I do think West Virginia writers have not been given the publicity they are due. I think they are overlooked."

Unfortunately, the stereotypes about residents of West Virginia still exist, and they apply to writers as well as the rest of the population. Nancy cites one example that occurred during an in-state writers' workshop. The teacher was from Virginia and admitted at the conclusion of the workshop that he was surprised that he found everyone in the group to be good writers when he had expected poor writing to be the norm.

"There are some excellent writers in West Virginia," Nancy says emphatically, "but some need help, and grants like ORBI can put them in touch with other writers and help build their confidence in what they're doing."

The primary ORBI grant is limited to $3,000 and is available to community groups and arts organizations. The legislatures of both West Virginia and Ohio require that these type grants be awarded only to those who provide matching funds for their projects. There are specific deadlines for the applications, and the overriding requirement — regardless of the artistic merits of the project — is that it actively involve artists, audiences, and communities on both sides of the Ohio River.

"We were meeting ORBI requirements before we knew ORBI existed. It's almost like ORBI was created with us in mind." Mack Lichterman, President of the Board of Directors, is talking about the River Cities Symphony. The symphony is headquartered in Parkersburg, West Virginia, but it draws members, volunteers, and financial support from across the river in Marietta, Ohio as well and presents half of its concerts there.

"When we first found out about ORBI, we felt we fit into what ORBI was trying to do as far as supporting groups that really were from the border communities in West Virginia and Ohio. What we were doing was a perfect match with that."

The River Cities Symphony is in its ninth season. Typical grants received from ORBI have supported the presentation of young peoples' concerts at high schools in the Parkersburg, West Virginia area and across the river in Marietta, Ohio. These were included in the Symphony's regular season of performance.

Lichterman is transplanted to West Virginia from Rochester, New York. He met his wife (a Marietta native) in a kibbutz in Israel. He has a degree in accounting from Ohio University, and after working for a while in Rochester, he and his wife decided to return to her home base in Appalachia. Mack is happy with his decision to live in Parkersburg, but there are situations in the region that alarm and disappoint him.

"I think the primary issue in the Mid-Ohio Valley is the lack of string programs in the school system, the lack of new symphonies. There are no school orchestral programs; they're long gone. Schools have reduced their funding in order to support marching bands. I don't have anything against marching bands, but I am appalled at the amount of resources that go into that as opposed to having a really good music education program. I think the kids are shortchanged when they don't have those programs."

Mack wants the Symphony to be the source of change for a situation that he thinks, if not addressed, will result in losing a generation of young people who could learn to appreciate and support symphonic music. "By having an orchestra that really serves the community, we can be the focal point for educational programs. There is great potential for our orchestra to serve education by having our musicians go out and teach in the schools. It will cost some money, but it is possible."

The ORBI grant is important to the River Cities Symphony in more ways than one. "It's $3,000, which is only one-thirtieth of our budget, but it's not chopped liver. It is important to us. The other side is that it validates what we do. When we go to ORBI, we're also going to the Ohio Arts Council and the West Virginia Commission on the Arts. ORBI validates what we do to these organizations as well."

Mack Lichterman did play with the orchestra (cello) when it first began, but as the orchestra became more professional, he felt he wasn't playing up to that same level, and he left to work tirelessly behind the scenes. He is an arts advocate with great plans for the future. "I envision an orchestra far beyond what we have today. This is just the beginning." The way Mack makes the statement, it's hard not to believe him.

As daunting as some individual artists and organization think the grant process is, Bill Howley assures those that he talks to that it is not. And he makes himself available to help simplify the process. As project director, he plays no role in award decision, but he will read drafts of applications and offer comments. The ORBI web site is also a source of information about requirements and deadlines.

Of course, Ohio-based arts organizations share in the ORBI grants as well. In the 2004 grant year, for instance, awards went to Harvey Firestone Park in Columbiana for summer concerts in the park and to the French Art Colony in Gallipolis for artist prizes for a juried gallery competition held during their annual River Recreation Festival. There is no reason to keep track of which side of the river receives the most grants, however, because the ORBI program is designed to benefit residents on both sides, regardless of which organization holds the grant.

In 1996, the Kootaga Indian Dancers applied for a grant to support a Native American Traditional Powwow in Belpre, Ohio. ORBI has provided part of the group's funding each year the group has applied since then. According to the organizers, their powwow in 1996 was the first full-scale powwow held in the Ohio River Valley. The goal of this annual festival is to promote a respect and understanding of the Native American cultures, arts, and customs, which have a rich heritage throughout West Virginia and Ohio.

The Kootaga Indian Dancers are twenty young men from Jackson and Wood County, West Virginia, and Washington and Athens County, Ohio. The group performs over twenty shows and seminars a year. Among the venues where they have showcased their talents, is the Ohio State Fair.

One aspect of the weekend event is the education of area youth in the culture of Native America. The dancers promote a school program Friday morning and a children's program Friday evening. Story telling, dancing, singing, face painting, crafts, flute playing, and Indian games are elements of the programming for this event.

Because of this authentic event and the awareness the Kootaga Indian Dancers have brought to the Ohio River Valley, there has been an increase in research by individuals to search for Native American bloodlines on family trees.

ORBI demonstrated a commitment to cultural and ethnic diversity from its inception. In its first grant year it funded an African American Jubilee celebration in Wheeling, West Virginia. The celebration was sponsored by Women Helping Youth (WHY) as a means of presenting art, drama, music, dance, food, culture, and history to the Upper Ohio River Valley. Its particular purpose was to help African American youth see and experience their heritage.

WHY, a coalition of concerned women, was organized to provide support and activities for at-risk youth. Their targets are the typically underserved minority and low-income communities. Through this program and others, the group hopes to stimulate self esteem and self determination.

The African American Jubilee celebration grew from a single-day event to a three-day celebration with a full range of activities such as drama, cultural and historic presentations, and storytelling.

African Americans have a long history in Appalachian Ohio, and this jubilee was one way to recognize and celebrate it and its significance to the rest of Appalachia.

"A bird doesn't sing because it has an answer;
it sings because it has a song."

Maya Angelou, Author, Poet, Playwright,
Educator, Actress

8

Afrilachians

B esides Native Americans who claim Appalachian heritage by virtue of their birth, African Americans have lived, worked, and practiced the arts — both traditional and contemporary — in the region for two hundred years. In the early years, most were former slaves, either runaways or those who had been freed. John Newton Templeton is most notable as being Ohio University's first black graduate (1828) and the fourth black person to graduate from college anywhere in the United States. Templeton was a former slave from South Carolina who lived and worked in the home of the college president. Ohio University, a model for diversity in the college education system, has taken another step forward by hiring the first black president in its two hundred-year history. Dr. Roderick J. McDavis, a Dayton native, is the first alumnus in 132 years to head the University.

It is the Ohio River farther south, though, that was the beacon for slaves coming into the region. They felt if they could just get across that river, freedom was theirs. Abolitionist John Rankin's house in Ripley was one of the first stops on the historic Underground Railroad. It's here that writer Harriet Beecher Stowe heard the story of an escaping slave carrying her baby across cakes of ice on the Ohio River in a desperate attempt to flee from slavery. The scene became part of her anti-slavery novel, *Uncle Tom's Cabin or Life Among the Lowly.* It's estimated that most of the two thousand slaves who crossed into Ohio stayed at the Rankin House. The Rankin House State Memorial and the Ripley Museum are part of Brown County's tourist attractions.

In the same area of Brown County is the John Parker Historic Site. Parker was a slave who purchased his own freedom and moved to a point across the Ohio River where he thought he and his family would be safe. From that location, Parker also helped fugitive slaves as a stop on the Underground Railroad, often crossing the river to Kentucky to lead the slaves across to safety. It's estimated that he helped nine hundred to one thousand slaves in their flight to freedom. Parker was also an iron manufacturer and an inventor. A tobacco press he designed is still in use today.

Michael Maloney explains how the former slave population began to settle into Southern Ohio. "So Ohio had many different migration points that created pockets of people: The French in Gallipolis is an example. Swiss in one area, Welsh in another. Including former slaves who, when they got their freedom, came to Ohio."

Beverly Warfield was surprised when she began learning about the slaves that settled along the river. "Those of us who didn't have knowledge of slave history in this country — and most African Americans don't because it's not taught in the schools — many of us thought that not many slaves settled in Ohio because it really was not a safe state. It was right across the river, and they could still come and get you. So our thinking was most slaves went up to Canada, to New York, to Massachusetts, and not many stayed there. But we learned — I learned through this process — that there were free slaves who were working right across the river in Ohio as part of the Underground Railroad. And these areas and communities valued that, and the white Appalachians in those communities were developing programs and arts around that information and those sites.

"It was really an eye opener to me," Beverly continues, "but when you talk to some of the black Appalachians, they can give you some real history on their families. They have been descendents of those people who have stayed."

A term is being used to identify the Appalachian heritage of those descendents. It's Afrilachian. Frank X. Walker, a multidisciplinary artist from Kentucky, takes credit for coining the word at a writing conference in Lexington a decade ago. Only he spelled the term "Affrilachian." An African American artist and activist, Walker says that he saw in a dictionary the definition of "Appalachian" as a "white resident of Appalachia." Knowing the term to be exclusive, he felt "Affrilachian" was more relevant to the Appalachian experience today. The term caught on and is in common use, but, for what ever reason, it is most often spelled with one *f* as Afrilachian.

Michael Maloney says the term is not derogatory but one that includes African Americans into the Appalachian heritage. "I'd say among the poets and writers, it's acceptable. It's not derogatory. In fact, the first time I heard it used was by an African American poetry group."

Beverly Warfield responds to hearing the term: "It was my first exposure. I had never heard the term until then. I never realized there were African American Appalachians, and I don't think most African Americans realize that there are African American Appalachians. Where you're born has a lot to do with who you are and what you are. Although I sensed that there was acceptance in their community of who they were and what they were, they were trying very hard to introduce the African roots and their African culture into the arts programs that their organizations were going to be presenting. They were interested in celebrating things like Juneteenth."

"In Cincinnati and Dayton, when we have someone like the Afrilachian Poets," says Michael Maloney, "we get a lot of response. There is also a demand and a need for interracial kinds of programming because race relations are a lot more important in the big cities."

It was a dedication to the idea that the Ohio Appalachian Arts Initiative would be diverse and include all people of Appalachian heritage that drove the thinking of the consultants. "As we sat down together and initially started planning the process," Beverly says, "we all kind of threw our cards out on the table as to how we wanted to proceed, and we designed what we thought would be a very inclusive process."

It's that inclusive process that has helped bring recognition to Afrilachian humorist and storyteller, Omope Carter Daboiku. Born in Ironton, and with a degree in sociology and cultural geography, Omope now lives in the College Hill neighborhood of Cincinnati. She has been affiliated with the Ohio Arts Council's Arts in Education program since 1990 and has performed on radio, in movies, and television, most notably for the PBS program "Mountain

Shadow: Four Appalachian Women Artists." Her reputation as a story teller led to her selection to be part of the Urban Appalachian Council's "Perceptions of Home," partially funded by the Ohio Appalachian Arts Initiative.

Like Michael Maloney and Michael London, she is an exile, a small-town person living in a city. She says she had trouble being an urban mother until someone pointed out to her that she was really a country girl. She realized that for transplants "Home" is where you want to be buried. She's planning on going back to Ironton to be buried and isn't bothered that the cemetery is still essentially segregated. "The people I know are all there together," she says.

9

The Initiative
Continues to Build

A key objective during the three years of the Ohio Appalachian Arts Initiative was not to reinvent things but to build on the foundation that already existed. Michael Maloney explains: "There were existing people, organizations, and institutions doing things, and we built on that existing structure. We weren't starting from scratch, because the Ohio Arts Council, extension people (OSU), and my organization had been into these things for a long time."

A survey conducted by the team of consultants was very important in taking this next step in developing a program.

"The survey and the public meetings were how we found out what the people wanted," Maloney stresses, "and because we had key people involved in both the survey and public meetings, we had full cooperation of the communities and the arts organizations. We didn't have the kind of resistance that usually happens when an outside organization comes into a community and tries to do something. We did it right. At those advisory meetings, people had a sense of empowerment. Anyone who knows anything about Appalachia knows that if you try to impose something from the outside, people greatly enjoy trashing it."

Michael London follows up on that idea: "Not only was there no resistance, there was just a sense of relief, a welcoming relief because they were part of it. And because of the real sense of empowerment, people didn't expect everything to happen overnight."

It's a good thing, because there was a lot of hard work ahead, but the team was buoyed by support from the Ohio Arts Council and Wayne Lawson's vision of helping artists and arts agencies see the same things in themselves that others do.

Michael London feels much of the credit for the Initiative's early success is due Michael Maloney. "Wayne acted as a visionary for this agency, and Michael was able to do that for this Initiative. His concept of empowerment and help and assistance was a good match with what this agency and the Minority Arts Program had already established. You almost can't help but have success with something like that."

Barbara Bayless says, "I see the Ohio Arts Council a lot of times as the organization that kind of brings folks together. We do it all the time. We know all these individual organizations, and a lot of times, they don't really know each other."

This wasn't accomplished from Columbus, though. The OAAI team got to know organizations as well as they did by setting up and working out of a field office.

The consultant mix changed at the end of the planning year. Beverly Warfield reduced the time she worked on the project but made herself available to work as needed for the Ohio Arts Council. She was involved in pursuing NEA funding for the Initiative and writing the follow-on reports that were required. The Initiative needed a field office to serve the Appalachian communities, and Michael Maloney was able to secure office space at Chatfield College in St. Martin, Ohio, located in Brown County. Michael was teaching there and had set up an Appalachian field office in that location for Catholic Social Services of the Diocese of Cincinnati. He would continue as lead project consultant for the Initiative, supervising a program coordinator who was to be hired. Michael London would also continue as a consultant, providing his organizational management and Arts-in-Education expertise to the program.

Melanie Warman, was hired in January of 1995 as program coordinator. She had a BFA in fine arts and previously had served as performing arts curator at the Southern Ohio Museum and was past president of the Portsmouth Area Arts Council. With management experience in the arts, she brought good communications skills to the team. This was an important asset, since one of the early goals was to develop a system of communication among the diverse artists and arts organizations in the region. Melanie became editor of the OAAI newsletter.

Good news followed in March of 1995 with the approval of an NEA grant of approximately $200,000 to fund the remaining two years of the Initiative. OAC was obligated to provide $53,000 per year. Additional fund-raising was required to complete budget needs. It was the fund-raising part of the coordinator's job that eventually proved difficult for Melanie. She recognized that she did not have the required abilities in this area and resigned in the fall of 1996, returning to other arts consulting projects in Portsmouth.

Michael London thinks part of the problem was that Melanie tended to have a more local concept of the Initiative while the rest of the team's vision was more global. "When we thought of Appalachian Ohio, we really had a big picture in our head that included urban Appalachia, that included small towns, that included folks that lived in Columbus and Cleveland. A real mix and very multi-level. With Melanie, I think there was a little bit of disconnect and a mismatch when we looked at the bigger picture of serving."

Regardless of the reason, it just wasn't the right fit needed to advance the Initiative, and Melanie moved on. Michael London took over as editor of the newsletter and made some important changes. "Originally we weren't able to get substantive input or distribution." He solved that problem by drafting anyone who was available to help as reporters or editors. He wrote some of the pieces himself and selected previously published stories from other sources. He coordinated the newsletter and did the layout.

"We asked ourselves what do people need to know about Appalachian Arts and took that and put it into a comfortable format for people to read, and then we found a way to get it to them that we could afford. Our whole focus was to ask: how do we communicate with people in rural areas? We communicate through our organizations, our networks."

Distribution, then, was the key to increasing circulation. Instead of being mailed to individual addresses, the newsletters went in bulk to schools, libraries, Chambers of Commerce, and to all the marketing and arts organizations for distribution to their membership. "We had great feedback, because people started seeing it," London says.

London points out that the newsletter and the artists directory are as close as the Appalachian Arts Initiative gets to active programs. In an interview for *Rural Report: The Newsletter of Rural Action*, he said, "Our role is not out front doing high profile programming, but providing support instead through networking, technical assistance, referrals, making connections, etc. We don't do *for* people; we do *with* people."

10

A Jolt of Energy
for the Program

Donna Sue Groves began taking up some of the slack caused by Melanie Warman's departure. She'd been introduced to the Ohio Arts Council's effort to develop Appalachian Arts while working as a VISTA volunteer for Ohio Parents for Drug Free Youth. Now OAAI received an opportunity for a VISTA through Rural Action, an organization seeking solutions to various problems in Appalachia. Donna Sue was asked to fill the spot working at Chatfield College, with a focus on art and Appalachian heritage. She gladly accepted the position and began working with the team.

What a break for the Initiative. They were providing office space at Chatfield College and paying Donna Sue mileage, and, in return, got a woman who approached each task with an enthusiasm and passion that seem to scream to all of Appalachian Ohio, "I am a blessed woman. Doing work I love, with people I love, in an area I love!"

Donna Sue's feelings for her "home" were exceptionally strong. She would talk to anyone about them, and she expressed them in a piece she wrote. This is the beginning:

Appalachia!

That word alone makes my heart
swell with pride and comfort.
I come from a lineage of folks
who took pride in their surroundings,
who managed to survive, who handed down
strengths, virtues, and dreams to me.
And I leave it to those who come after me ....
The mountains and the valleys
of what is called Appalachia
will always be my home
and my bliss to me!

West Virginia was Donna Sue's childhood home. She grew up in Kanawha County on the Elk River. She followed five generations of strong, determined individuals who survived the hardships of the Appalachian Region.

Donna Sue had no formal training in the arts but looks back at her Girl Scout experience to see how the arts could teach, entertain, and integrate groups. She says, "Girl Scouts was the key to a diversity of experiences and learning to give back and to share. Having been a Girl Scout in the '50s and '60s, gave me a choice of something other than drugs."

She became a Girl Scout leader while a student at West Virginia University, traveling by bus to Thurman, a coal-mining town, to organize and meet with girls who had very few activities of value available to them. She worked through the Girl Scout organization to build their self-esteem.

Besides being an advocate, Donna Sue found herself drawn to political activism during that same period of time. She protested the war in Viet Nam and marched in the War on Poverty. She would be thrust into this role again in the early '80s when she was living in Xenia, Ohio. Her home was in a working-class neighborhood, and she became increasingly frustrated with the lack of city services the area was receiving. She organized that end of town into a coalition and eventually led a group to a meeting of the City Commissioners and was able to extract a promise to pave the streets in the area, a much-needed service to residents.

That success led her community to ask her to run for City Commissioner. She accepted and started a campaign that carried her door to door, talking to the people. She won, beating an incumbent. She was the youngest female ever elected to that position.

Although her unwillingness to compromise her positions made it difficult to be an effective advocate, being elected and working as a City Commissioner did provide a big boost to Donna Sue's self-esteem. However, frustrated with her inability to accomplish her goals as a City Commissioner, she left the position before her term expired and moved with her mother, a retired school teacher, to Adams County.

The first assignment Donna Sue worked to complete for the Initiative was to update the *Directory of Appalachian Arts in Ohio*. The initial printing of the directory in the mid '80s, although useful in identifying individual artists and arts organization in the region, was certainly not the definitive list, and, consequently, was not the information resource that it was capable of being. Donna Sue points out that in Adams County, her home, the only entry was radio station WRAC. It played bluegrass once a week for thirty minutes. She knew that a lot of hard work needed to be done, and she used the project as an opportunity to get out into the communities and engage people. "Getting artists to fill out a form from the government — the Ohio Arts Council — was a difficult thing, but it sure opened up a way for me to communicate with people."

Donna Sue was quickly able to build trust, the first step in the process of getting people to start talking about themselves and their art. "That takes a lot of relation building. Especially with individual artists to get them to talk about what's nearest and dearest and most precious to their souls, and that's their creative self."

It might have been like pulling teeth at times, but the hard work Donna Sue did in the region paid off. "Watching people grab that directory was wonderful," she says. "They just couldn't wait. And they would read it over and over and look at it again. Nothing ever changed in it, but they would see their neighbor's name, maybe see themselves, and it was just a way of validating themselves."

One of the problems that Donna Sue encountered in creating the artist directory was one that had been identified early on during the year of fact finding and evaluation. It had to do with image. Many individual artists in the Appalachian region simply didn't think of themselves as artists.

Barbara Summers, Executive Director of the Southern Hills Arts Council in Jackson County, tells a story that illustrates the thinking. She was complimenting a man who had carved from wood a gorgeous bird with a three-foot wingspan. His reply: "Oh, it's just whittlin'." He felt he was just doing what he'd seen others in his family do before him. He might have been carrying on an Appalachian tradition, but he had no idea it was considered art.

"It's the Appalachian demeanor, I think," says Linda Basye, Executive Director of the Pike County Convention and Visitors Bureau. "It's that mindset that what they do is not of value because it's what they've always done. They made their own quilts as covers for warmth because they couldn't afford to buy them. And yet now that's considered a true art form, but they've always done this, so it's not a big deal."

Beverly Warfield remembers discussing the subject in the earliest meetings with artists and arts organizations. "I think some of the biggest issues, the greatest conversations, centered around the difference between fine art and folk art. By letting people who were involved as the producers of the art and who were the developers of the programs really listen to each other and talk about the differences, I saw people's eyes just kind of open instead of glossing over, and they became interested in pursuing the possibilities of what could happen if people were exposed to all kinds of art."

Donna Sue admits that preconceived ideas of what constituted art clouded her own thinking on the subject. She hadn't originally thought of such activities as weaving, quilting, or playing the dulcimer as art and had to have her awareness raised in this area before she could convince others of their talent. Eventually she was able to get that message through to her own mother, Maxine Groves, a master quilter who had learned the craft from her mother and had a local reputation for her quality work. Donna Sue finally convinced her that she needed to start signing the back of her art as a painter might sign a canvas. Today her reputation as a quilter has grown to regional and beyond.

With the *Directory of Appalachian Arts in Ohio* project underway, Donna Sue went to the team with a proposal. If she continued working as a VISTA for Rural Action but also took over Melanie Warman's job (the departed field coordinator), "would you consider hiring me?" she asked. To her surprise, the response was "Sure." She quickly negotiated a laptop computer and a secretary to relieve her of the burden of the necessary correspondence and other paperwork. Donna Sue Groves was officially part of the Appalachian Arts Initiative team, and the people in every area that she touched with her gentle hand, hard work, and fierce Appalachian pride became the beneficiaries.

11

Building the Next Generation

The key to building a next generation of Appalachian residents who would appreciate their traditional arts as well as give their own artistic talents gladly to their communities was thought to be in developing art in the schools. Unfortunately, the team discovered that arts education was lacking in the schools of the region. Local arts organizations were trying to help, and the Ohio Arts Council thought it could lend a hand with its Arts in Education Program.

OAAI team leader Michael Maloney calls the Arts in Education Program "a perfect match. Part of our task was to get the services of the Ohio Arts Council to an underserved area, so it was fortunate for the Initiative that here you had an Arts Council that wanted to expand its program and its constituency to traditional arts. And these kids in schools will be able to feel better about themselves and their heritage. So it was a perfect match, both conceptually and institutionally."

Christy Farnbauch, then assistant coordinator of the Arts in Education Program at the Ohio Arts Council, was responsible for introducing the program in Appalachian Ohio. She was a young woman who had joined the OAC in 1991. Christy had earned a Bachelor of Arts degree — graduating with honors — from Otterbein College three years earlier. Her major was music business and trumpet performance with a minor in business administration. Prior to joining the Ohio Arts Council, she worked for three years as executive director of the Ohio Arts Presenters Network (OAPN), splitting time between Rio Grande/Gallipolis and Columbus. Today she continues to showcase her musical talent as a freelance musician.

Born in Marietta in Washington County, Christy was Appalachian by birth and upbringing but admits she had not thought of herself in that way. It was only during visits to Ohio State and Otterbein while she was trying to make a college selection did the subject really enter her mind. She discovered that by virtue of the location of her birth, she was eligible for an Appalachian scholarship. With this reminder of her heritage, she began to become more aware of her roots and the values that motivated her. After working in Appalachia for OAPN, Christy had a pretty good idea of the needs of the region in terms of the arts. They wanted more art in their schools. The OAAI had also determined that in their early explorations.

Michael Maloney says that the Arts in Education Program was an important element. "Christy came in loaded and ready to go. One of the things they (parents) said was that they wanted to have residencies in their schools. We focused on that and laid out a very specific plan with bench marks."

Working with the Initiative team, Christy set a goal to bring six schools a year into the Arts in Education Program, a total of eighteen for the three-year period. The program's approach was to do a lot of hand holding as the schools selected artists, applied for the residencies, and set about meeting the matching funds requirement.

Barbara Bayless recalls that she and Christy went to the schools to help the planning committees write their drafts and to go over them and discuss with them what was important, what the panels focused on.

"It was amazing to me the pride that people took in their residency effort," Christy says. "They really wanted to raise the money or they'd find a place for the artists to live and stay while they were in town." The Artist Directory for the Arts in Education Program was the source for identifying the types of artist and locating them.

"We did a lot of traveling and hand holding and reading their drafts and helping them write, and when the applications came through, the panelists knew that they had to be a little more understanding because of how we were trying to build up residencies in the region," Christy remembers.

Donna Sue Groves explains what this approach by the Ohio Arts Council was intended to accomplish: "It's not doing for someone; it's giving them the tools, the opportunities. Being their voice until they find their own voices."

The program was successful in meeting its goal of bringing artist residencies to eighteen schools in Ohio's Appalachian region. "It was a good entry point into the arts in those communities," Christy says. "It was an easy way to get the parents involved and the kids excited."

Beverly Warfield agrees. "We did see people who could begin to think of art as a cultural expression that could change the lives of children, and that was a very definite aspect of the program. Sometimes people look at art as just art; it's just something for the kids to do, some hands-on activity. That thinking began to change once they heard the artist talk about the changes that art involvement makes in children's lives and their exposure to art and how it can develop into a lifetime learning experience or potentially an employment opportunity if you identify a skill that someone can go on to develop. They began to understand that it was a way that people can carry on a cultural presence in their community and outside of their community that they hadn't ever thought about before."

What also changed, Christy Farnbauch says, is the viewpoint that the Arts in Education Program was for schools only. The program had been structured for kindergarten through the twelfth grade, requiring the residency to happen during the school day and year. The Appalachian Arts Initiative wanted to expand that thinking. Christy says, "We asked, 'What about a summer program at a Y?' What about at the library? What about at a community college?' Now we were talking about school and non-school residencies." The Initiative team had some new directions to turn to with their arts program for Appalachian children.

Other programs that had an impact on children as well as entire communities were the Perceptions of Home traveling display and performances by a stage group from Kentucky called Roadside Theater.

Taking advantage of the Perceptions of Home project was one of the first things the Initiative team did. The $70,000 project was already in work by the

Urban Appalachian Council, and OAAI provided some funding to help complete the work. It was a large display consisting of a series of tri-fold panels that could be setup kiosk style. There were photographs and biographies of individuals from Appalachian backgrounds who had succeeded in various walks of life, including such arts-related occupations as folk singers or woodcarvers.

"It fit so well with our goals, that we made it a premier project," says Michael Maloney. "It was all about recognizing Appalachians for their accomplishments. Of course, in the process, it countered the stereotypes."

In like manner, Roadside Theater dealt with themes of pride in culture. It was an out-of-state theater group but used regional terminology to connect with its audience. By providing some funding and helping to provide venues for performances, the OAAI enjoyed a dual benefit: people were exposed to the artistic expression of live theater while also receiving positive messages about their culture.

Oral histories, as a method of communicating existing values to the young people, were also suggested by the residents of Appalachian Ohio. Michael London remembers that the Initiative team worked to discover if anyone in the region was involved in developing oral histories and determined that Rural Action had someone who was doing that. The group did provide funding to one senior citizens center in

Portsmouth to write the stories of their residents in a collection called "Memory Makers." The development of a murals project was thought to be an excellent way to involve community citizens with school children and to get people thinking about their oral histories in the process.

"If I could say it in words,
there would be no reason to paint."

Edward Hopper, Painter and Engraver

12

Using Art in the Present to Explore the Past and the Future

In many cultures, the painting of public murals has long been an accepted practice, not only to illustrate the history of a community, but also to express hope for its future. Since the days of a cave society, important events, such as a successful hunt or winning a major battle over a fierce enemy, have been depicted in a community display. Storytellers would use the paintings — sometimes no more than primitive scrawls on the wall of a cave — to recount past glories so that the tribe would not lose touch with its heritage. It was this purpose that drove the OAAI team to promote and assist communities in the development of mural projects. The Ohio Arts Council and ORBI promoted mural projects on both sides of the river.

Michael Maloney describes the mural project as another perfect fit with the goals of the Ohio Appalachian Arts Initiative because it attempts to involve the whole community in developing images that support the history or future aspirations of a town. Typically, people would get together and begin to recount the history of their community as they searched for images that they wanted to depict. An artist would be chosen to work with school children in developing the images, while community merchants might donate supplies or provide a location for the mural that had good access and visibility in the community. The actual painting would be done by the artist or by volunteers under the direction of the artist. Once the mural was complete, an unveiling ceremony introduced it to the larger community, usually with a celebration of accomplishment that might include other artistic expressions such as music.

Among the murals sponsored in part by the OAAI and the Ohio Arts Council was one in Perry County and one in Athens County. The Perry County mural was painted on two sides of a brick building housing the Shawnee Village Restaurant in downtown Shawnee. It's based on drawings and poetry done by local school children and reflects the memories, hopes, fears, and frustrations of the community.

In Athens County, the mural was painted on the cinder block wall of the Trimble High School cafeteria. The painting is a collage of images gathered by the art students and represents landmarks, people, and events important to the community.

A Heritage mural, sponsored in part by the Ohio Arts Council and the Ohio River Border Initiative, was developed in Meigs County. It's painted on a brick wall of the City National Bank in Pomeroy and represents four important aspects of the region: the Ohio River, agriculture, industry, and architecture.

In Coshocton, a city in one of Appalachian Ohio's eastern counties, the mural project that was conceived and executed serves a purpose beyond an association with the historical representation of the area. It was designed to help children identify and confront their fears. It's called "Protecting Our Children," and it was conceived and executed by the Pomerene Center for the Arts and funded by the Gannet Foundation and the Ohio Appalachian Arts Program.

The Pomerene Center for the Arts is housed in an 1836 Greek Revival home previously owned by the founders of the museum in nearby Roscoe Village. The center includes five art galleries available for exhibits from local, regional, and national artists. It also sponsors a variety of art-related classes.

Anne Cornell is the center's fourth director. She describes herself as a dilettante when it comes to her interest in the arts but, in talking to her, it becomes obvious that her background is more varied and well rounded than superficial. She attended Kenyon College for a year before leaving to pursue her education in the arts in other parts of the country and overseas. She studied piano in Germany for a year and a half and also paints.

The mural idea grew from a Pomerene Center for the Arts summer program for six- to fourteen-year-old children called Angels, Superheroes, and Fantastic Beasts. The children were asked the question, "If you could create your own guardian, what would it look like?" The images that resulted were the starting point for the mural project.

"The project was conceived in a climate where we are often afraid for our own kids," Anne Cornell says. "And with the war going on, we carry fear around with us. "Whether consciously or not, fear is a big part of what goes on in us. So this project was envisioned to inspire a community dialogue about fears and about the very simple ways we protect ourselves."

Anne thinks that the use of a mural in this role reflects how important art is in expressing ideas in a public way. "It's very much the role of the arts," she emphasizes.

The lead artist selected for the mural project was a Russian-born woman named Marianna Smith who came to Columbus to complete graduate work at the Columbus College of Art and Design (CCAD). Her helping artists were eight fourteen- to eighteen-year-old students, three of whom joined the group from a work program at the Coshocton Behavioral Health Center. The artist worked with her assistants for a month on the project, getting them to identify their fears in visual terms. Work on the mural was integrated with a mask-making project to serve as visual models for the figures' faces.

During the mural project, Anne saw first-hand the ability of art to open avenues of dialogue and understanding between people, especially those from different backgrounds. One of the young helpers from the Behavioral Health Center was a wannabe skinhead, she relates, and he quickly confronted the artist. "Are you a communist?" he wanted to know. The artist wasn't threatened by his question or those that followed. She patiently and calmly answered all of them. She was very open about her ideas and willing to engage him about his beliefs. The two set up a dialogue, Anne relates, and developed a mutual respect for each other by project end.

"We are very monochrome here [in Coshocton]," Anne says. "We're almost devoid of any color or ethnic variations and pretty closed experience-wise, so to have someone come in who was from a socialistic background and to exchange ideas peacefully is something."

The project consists of five painted panels featuring artwork, plus two panels of text. They cover six windows and a doorway of the Fisher Decorating Center, a downtown building that Anne describes as "really ugly." The panels were cut to size, painted, and then installed on one outside wall of the building. The paintings consist of a variety of images in intense colors, using silhouettes for the bodies and primitive type masks for the faces. "But it's not meant to be confrontational or in-your-face," Anne says. "The elementary kids who had figures on here are tremendously proud. Everyone who worked on it has a real sense of ownership in it. They are glad to have their names on it."

Coshocton has several murals in the community, and now Protecting Our Children takes its place as public display of the arts with the others. "The whole idea of a mural is that it's there," Anne says. "You just see it without making an effort. You assimilate it somehow, and if there's enough information, you might hear how others are thinking about it."

Anne Cornell and the Pomerene Center for the Arts have been hearing about this mural. "This has led to, as you can imagine, quite a lot of dialogue because it's not altogether benign. It's a little scary. There've been some interesting conversations around it. We've talked to people about the development of it and gotten responses about the piece and comments about not only what you do in public

Center and Two Right Panels of Mural "Protecting Our Children"
Lead Artist —Marianna Smith

Using Art in the Present to Explore the Past and the Future • 93

spaces but also just the potential of art in a community setting."

The responses from surveys conducted of residents of Coshocton who viewed the mural, while generally favorable, are as varied as the members of the community itself:

- "Bold colors make a bold statement about people and the lives they lead; a seeming mystery. Nonetheless, the work is really appreciated. Thanks for making Coshocton more rich."
- "A really great way for kids to express themselves. Unique and artistic."
- "The piece is too dark for that age group, for Christians."
- "Very interesting piece of artwork! Adds a pleasing eye catcher!"
- "I don't understand what it is. I read it was about angels watching over kids. I don't see that at all by looking at it."
- "I didn't understand the meaning, but I liked it."
- "It was a very unique idea. More paintings should be done throughout the city. Awesome!"

That people were engaged by this mural is strong testimony to the success of the project. The French philosopher Voltaire said, "It's not sufficient to see and know the beauty of a work, we must feel and be affected by it."

"When you stop having dreams and ideals —
well you might as well stop altogether."

Marion Anderson, Singer

13

From Initiative to Program

A fter three years of successful development in a region that covers over fourteen thousand square miles and is home to more than 1.4 million residents, the Ohio Appalachian Arts Initiative team took stock of what had been accomplished.

Wayne Lawson thinks the Ohio Arts Council did a lot of things right. "It was obvious people in Appalachia don't want government telling them what to do. We didn't do that. I think there's a mutual respect that's grown up between us representing a government agency and people in Appalachia."

Barbara Bayless gives a lot of credit to the fact that the Initiative maintained a strong presence in the field. "In the early days," she says, "Wayne always talked about the Ohio Arts Council being accessible to the community, and when we've talked about programs, it's really about going out into the field. The value to me is to see how people are successful in what we've been able to help them with."

Michael London agrees wholeheartedly. "The single most important thing that has happened — based on the voice that was given at the beginning of this process — is the fact that the agency has personal representation in the field, and if everything else stops, I would maintain that that would still be the most significant impact of anything regardless of funding any activity because of the access that it gives. And it is access that comes from personal relationships that are developed by picking up the phone and calling someone from your area — who knows your area — who understands who you are, who you can really meet with. That is so critical to the process. It says even if this doesn't get funded and that doesn't get funded, we'll be back. And Donna Sue's presence in the region is evidence of that, so there's trust."

Donna Sue Groves thinks the tools that were created by the team to assess the needs of the communities played a big role in what was accomplished. "I think the survey was a very important tool. And the work we fashioned was using that tool that was based on what the community said were their needs."

"It was such a wonderful program because it really wasn't about us," Beverly Warfield remembers. "It really wasn't about the Arts Council except as a funding source and a way to access additional funds. It was basically about the needs of this great community and the lack of artistic opportunities and exposure for the children."

"People didn't hesitate to call us on things we weren't doing well," Michael Maloney says, "but because we were listening that didn't happen a lot. They knew that funding was always limited and that staff was always limited, so we moved slowly, but no one ever really jumped us because they were part of the process. They knew we were working our tails off."

Linda Basye, Executive Director of the Pike County Travel and Visitors Bureau agrees. "There is a lot of art in Appalachian Ohio that would not be here without the support of the Ohio Arts Council and their foresight to establish this program. They have done so much to pump up the artists in this area. It's phenomenal what they've done in a short period of time, really."

Michael London says, "If you just look at the data — assuming we have no anecdotal information — if you just look at the data we have in this agency, if you just look at what it was ten years before the

OAAI, and what it was ten years after, that alone should tell the story."

"It's so easy to see how it's grown by leaps and bounds because of how underserved it was," Michael Maloney adds. "Looking back over my lifetime of work, it's one of the things I'm really proud of."

The transition from Initiative to Program has specific steps that must be followed.

Wayne Lawson explains the process: "It's simple. You field test it, discuss it with as many people as possible, then take it to the board and sell them. Get board approval. And something I didn't mention that I think is very important is that we've had such good representation on the board. That has meant a lot."

The Ohio Arts Council received some help in this Initiative-to-Program transition by being recognized for the good job it had done in the region. "The shift of political power in the state from Cleveland to Appalachia brought the program to prominence," Wayne says. "The new legislature could ignore us but not the work we were doing. We didn't need a mandate; we were already there. We were doing what we were supposed to be doing, and I wager that helped us immensely."

The Initiative-to-Program transition was not without its ups and downs. There was a time, Barbara Bayless says, when the Ohio Arts Council considered cutting Appalachian Arts loose and letting it develop as an independent program in the region, responsible for its own funding and administration.

"I took Wayne down to Chatfield College," Barbara remembers, "and we all met — Michael Maloney, Michael London, Donna Sue, Wayne, and I — and at that time, he wanted us to think about becoming a separate program and go out and raise our own money. He was considering pushing the program out. Then he brought it back in and made it part of OAC."

Wayne Lawson says that the expense of so many consultants working in different parts of the state did cause him to wonder why the group couldn't do some fund-raising and create their own entity. "That idea didn't last long when I considered that it would be better run if we centralized it in our own agency," he says. "Indeed, that was the way to go when you look at the success of it now."

As the Initiative moved to the Program stage, key consultants Michael Maloney and Michael London left the critical, active roles they had played in the process and returned to being available for general consulting with the Ohio Arts Council. The office was closed at Chatfield College, and Donna Sue Groves was left to serve the southern region from a home-based office.

Commenting on her new status, Donna Sue says, "One of the great things for me personally has been the opportunity to be mentored by the finest professionals, from Michael Maloney, to Barbara Bayless, to Michael London, to Christy Farnbauch, and to the visionary, Wayne Lawson, thinking so far out there.

Where in the world in my lifetime could this have happened?"

As far as a personal philosophy to guide her in the job at hand, Donna Sue was quoted in the Autumn 2003 newsletter of *Ohio Designer Craftsmen* as saying: "I would like to reinforce the positives and gifts of the Ohio Appalachian region. Instead of talking about what we do not have, how poor we are, how bad the unemployment rate is, I want to hear us say, 'Did you know that we are number one in this, that we have the most of that, or that we are the best at this?' Turn our thoughts into positive images and positive action." And the vehicle she would use to accomplish these objectives would be promotion of the arts in Appalachia.

14

And More Change

During this transition phase from Initiative to Program, there were other changes going on at the Ohio Arts Council that would sooner or later impact the Ohio Appalachian Arts Program. The first began with the establishment in 1997 of a Community Development Initiative (CDI). This Initiative was a pilot project designed to demonstrate strategic ways that arts can be connected to core community values and everyday life. Its goal was to develop economic, educational, and cultural partnerships that would position the arts at the center of community development.

Christy Farnbauch moved from the Arts in Education Program to be coordinator of the new Initiative. Speaking of Wayne Lawson's selection of her to head the Initiative, Christy says, "He saw in me something I didn't see in myself, and it was challenging."

Christy took hold of her new position by changing the way community cultural planning had previously been done in the field. In the old model, local arts councils surveyed a selected number of people who were familiar with the organization and it's programming and then wrote a cultural plan for the community. Results tended to be the same in each location. Every community needed more performance space and increased funding for the arts.

Christy explains the new approach: "Our model started with the community. We hired teams of three [individuals] who were not arts people, but rather community planners. They were asked to complete research about the hopes, fears, dreams, and aspirations of community members. Then, they looked for ways to connect the arts as part of the solution."

Late in 2000, there was a major restructuring of programs at the Ohio Arts Council. Grants were written that would assist in moving the Ohio Appalachian Arts Program under the jurisdiction of Community Development. This included the Ohio River Border Initiative as well as community and folk festivals. Funding was made available in May of 2001, and Christy Farnbauch was promoted to Director.

Donna Sue Groves became a full-time employee of the Ohio Arts Council as part of the new organization. She was also appointed Southern Field Representative for the Ohio Arts Council along with her duties with the Appalachian Arts Program. She reported to Christy under the new organizational chart along with Bill Howley, part-time contractor serving as Project Director of ORBI.

The new arrangement made sense for the Ohio Arts Council, Christy says speaking about the agency's goal. "It certainly is about developing communities, not just representing minority communities." Since Christy is from the region, she felt she was a logical choice as team leader of the Ohio Appalachian Arts Program, and it fit Wayne Lawson's plan of connecting people and programs.

"I didn't hire her because she was from Appalachia," Wayne says. "Afterwards it made sense. That was just one more connect."

As the new millennium moved into full swing, The Ohio Appalachian Arts Program was in new hands but dedicated to continuing the service to the residents of Appalachian Ohio it had established ten years earlier.

"Art is not a study of positive reality,
it is the seeking of ideal truth."

George Sand, Novelist

15

Including OMEGA

The original target area for both the planning process and the Ohio Appalachian Arts Initiative was the nineteen-county region along the Ohio River from Brown County in the west to Washington County in the east. Funding was not available to include the other ten counties that formed a portion of the eastern border of the state.

Christy Farnbauch remembers the first major order of business for her as she began working with the Appalachian Arts Program: "I said how come we're only serving half of the region? I went to Wayne [Lawson], and he agreed." The program

*Ten Eastern Counties of Ohio Added to the Southern Nineteen as
Part of the Ohio Appalachian Arts Program (OAAP)*

needed to begin serving the eastern counties with the
same dedication that it was serving the southern
ones.

It was obvious that regardless of how hard Donna Sue worked, she couldn't do justice to twenty-nine counties. Besides the lack of budget, the distances involved were just too vast. Funding had to be made available and someone needed to be hired to concentrate service in the ten eastern counties referred to as OMEGA, (Ohio Mid-Eastern Government Association), a designation used by the Appalachian Regional Commission.

A job description was drawn up, and a writer who had returned to the area and was living in Coshocton was hired to fill the part-time position. There were some medical problems, however, and he soon realized that he wasn't going to be able to meet the expectations of the job and resigned.

The position was advertised in regional newspapers and, after interviewing several candidates, Caroline Pierson joined the team as Field Consultant, Northern Appalachia.

Caroline came to the program from Muskingum College where she was a grants officer. She grew up in the area and has a degree in theater from Dennison University. She has been assistant managing director of the Pritchard Laughlin Civic Center in Cambridge, and besides her jobs in the arts field, she has worked in the community as a volunteer in a number of arts related projects.

When she took the position, Caroline says there were not a lot of guidelines, but she understood her job to be acting as liaison between the communities and the artists, to offer the resources of the Ohio Arts Council to the communities, and to help communities understand how the arts impact them. She was to offer information, help build partnerships, pull groups together, and help arts organizations and people outside of the counties she served recognize the artists in her counties.

Donna Sue did help her get started, and the two continue to work together on various aspects of the program. The fact that the Ohio River Border Initiative did start its programs in the eastern region provided some help in establishing a base of individuals and organizations on which to begin building.

Although people living in Ohio's southern counties and its eastern counties are both Appalachian, there are some general differences. Southern counties are more rural and isolated with populations of Scots-Irish, Anglo-Saxon, or Pennsylvania German descent. In the eastern counties, there is more industrialization, and the Ohio River Valley is populated by many people of central and southern European descent: Italian, Polish, Hungarian, Russian, etc. There are also a higher number of African Americans.

"I work better with organizations and groups," Caroline says. "I think that's what I do best. One of the things I really enjoy seeing happen is building partnerships and helping people connect with other people. To offer opportunities for groups to work with other groups for bigger and better results."

Donna Sue Groves feels Caroline started her job with a handicap. "Caroline did not have the gift of being involved in the Initiative and seeing it develop from the beginning," she says. "What she's brought is wonderful organizational skills. Like her work with the Festivals Conference."

Christy Farnbauch thinks Caroline is the right personality and the right kind of person for the area. "In the last year, I think she's really blossomed, but it's taken awhile for her to understand — with Donna Sue coaching her — that you need to go to the meetings in the region; you need to keep showing up in places, meet with individual artists, go to festivals. Working independently from a home-based office was new to her. In the last year, she's been all over the place."

Caroline has seen the impact of the OAAP grants on individual artists and organizations in the region she serves. "The grants are only $2,000, but we have seen very important pilot programs, some very strong arts programming get off the ground. This is an opportunity to say, 'I can do this. I have some help, some people who believe in me.' A lot of times it will be a start, that impetus toward bigger things."

Sometimes the grant is a move toward self-sufficiency, to getting others involved artistically and financially, helping a program find a permanent home or date on a calendar. Caroline remembers such a story: "We were in Mingo Junction for one of the mural projects that didn't get off the ground, and I was talking to someone who was interested in doing summer music programs in the park, but he couldn't get a lot of people behind him, and he couldn't find the money. I said, 'Let's work on a plan to see if we can't get you a few dollars to do a pilot for the first year.' We got the money; he did the program, and it was a wild success.

"The next year it was getting close to the deadline, and I asked him if he wanted to work on applying for another grant, and he said, 'No. Thank you for the grant, but the town council discovered how much everyone liked the music, and they're going to fund it.' It's an $1,800 story; it's not a big money story, but it was important to the community."

What's also important to many eastern communities along the Ohio River is football. Martins Ferry is only eighteen miles south of Mingo Junction. Both communities sit on Ohio Route 7. James Wright, Ohio's most famous poet and Martins Ferry's favorite son, captures the industrial nature and the ethnic mix of the region as he writes about the importance of football in that part of the state.

Autumn Begins in Martins Ferry, Ohio

In the Shreve High football stadium,
I think of Polacks nursing long beers in Tiltonsville,
And gray faces of Negroes in the blast furnace at
   Benwood,
And the ruptured night watchman of Wheeling Steel,
Dreaming of heroes.

All the proud fathers are ashamed to go home.
Their women cluck like starved pullets,
Dying for love.

Therefore,
Their sons grow suicidally beautiful
At the beginning of October,
And gallop terribly against each other's bodies.

Surely the sons of Mingo Junction gallop terribly against each other's bodies in the fall as well, but in the summer — thanks to a kick-start from the Ohio Appalachian Arts Program — they listen to beautiful music in the park.

"Nobody is bored when he is trying to
make something that is beautiful,
or to discover something that is true."

William Inge, Author, Playwright

16

Taking the Message out of the Hollow and the Hills

A major objective of the Ohio Appalachian Arts Program is to help artists identify their crafts and, in turn, feel good about themselves as they begin to share their talents with others. It also has a goal of presenting a more positive image of the region to other residents of the state and, in fact, to the entire country.

"Media plays a big role in creating stereotypes," Michael Maloney says. "If you read the *Cincinnati Enquirer* and live where Donna Sue does [Adams County], you become aware that the *Cincinnati*

Enquirer thinks that we're a bunch of lazy welfare cheats, which doesn't fit at all, because most people wouldn't think of accepting welfare even if they were starving. Most Appalachians are very proud and would rather die than go on welfare."

It appears that there is still considerable work to be done — even in the region — to change the perceptions of Appalachian residents into the honest, proud, hardworking people that they are. Traveling displays, such as Perceptions of Home and the Athens Photographic Project help considerably in taking positive images of the region to locations outside.

Festivals are another source for producing interesting and positive images of the Appalachian culture and the regional location. In this case, attendees come to the region, listen to local music, sample good down-home cooking, and experience Appalachian art (both traditional and contemporary), and take their perceptions home with them. According to the National Endowment for the Arts, Ohio ranks second in the nation for attendance at art fairs and festivals. Obviously, the potential for making a positive impression is great, not to mention the economic value to the area through visitors who come from across the state, the nation, and even from foreign countries.

Maloney discovered years ago the capability of festivals to promote the notion that cultural heritage is important. He worked through the Urban Appalachian Council in Cincinnati to organize neighborhood festivals, as well as a city-wide Appalachian Festival that had preserving heritage at their core.

The OAAP and ORBI continue to support festival activities in the region. They were part of the Second Annual Appalachian Ohio Festivals Conference held at Hocking College in late March of 2004. Participants, realizing the importance of festivals and of the conference to successful festival planning, have embraced the idea of working together for the common good of the region. In a conference debriefing session in early May, representatives from festivals committees and arts organizations in the region reviewed what worked well and what could be changed to improve the festival experience for all Appalachians and the attendees. The Ohio Arts Council had three representatives present: Barbara Bayless, Coordinator of the Minority Arts Program; Donna Sue Groves, Appalachian Field Coordinator; and Caroline Pierson, Field Consultant, Northern Appalachia.

Caroline explains her thinking about the importance of festivals to the region. "I think from a cultural standpoint, they're incredibly important. I know people who come back year after year after year just to maintain contact with the people they've met. It's a chance for people who were born and raised here and have a house, a life somewhere else to come 'home' for awhile."

Appalachian writers who present accurate, vivid depictions of the region and its people are also good vehicles to counter the media's misrepresentations.

Danny Fulks is one of those writers. He is well known as an Appalachian storyteller. His tales, garnered from a life spent in Appalachia, are filled with accurate description and an insight into the hearts and minds of his fellow residents. Smoky beer joints, bluegrass and gospel music, preachers urging repentance at church revivals, families trying to scratch out a living farming tobacco, towns withstanding floods, and overcoming the many obstacles of daily life. These are the subjects of his stories.

Born on a farm in Gallia County, Fulks was a reader at an early age. He remembers his grandfather teaching him to read the labels on whiskey bottles when he was five. "I'm not saying my family was poor," Fulks recounts in a essay called, 'Foggy Riffs,' "but I remember reading newspapers that had been used as wallpaper. Read them right on the wall."

He worked at a variety of blue-collar jobs before becoming a teacher and school principal. He earned a Ph.D. from the University of Tennessee, is Professor Emeritus at Marshall University in West Virginia, and is currently an adjunct professor at Ohio University, Ironton branch. He resides in Huntington, West Virginia.

In an essay entitled, "The Way We Laughed," in his latest book, *Tragedy on Greasy Ridge: true stories from Appalachian Ohio*, Fulks relates Appalachian humor to the oral tradition. He tells a story about a barmaid thwarting the efforts of a man trying to carry a door into a beer joint in Wellsville, Ohio. Her salty language chases him right out of the bar, so the man leans the door against the wall outside, comes back into the bar, orders and drinks his beer, and continues on his way with the door.

"This is the kind of humor," Fulks writes, "that I have seen and heard many times while growing up in Appalachia. Short. Sharp. Irreverent. Deadpan. Hard times, death, poverty, and a general melancholy among the people would at times give way to irony. The humor I saw and heard was delivered with nuances, inflections, and nonverbal expressions impossible to convert to mere printed words. Not long, drawn-out tales or allegories. Not parables or epiphanies. Simple and spare, spur-of-the-moment comments and behaviors. Some, however, live on through the years as oral tradition."

"I work from awkwardness. By that I mean
I don't like to arrange things. If I stand in
front of something, instead of arranging it,
I arrange myself."

Diane Arbus, Photographer

17

True Stories of Appalachia

S tories abound in Appalachia, and it's through the tradition of storytelling — not in the numbers and data — that people begin to understand the impact of the arts in their lives.

Many of the stories are about individual and group projects that are made possible, or at least more successful, through funding received from the Ohio Appalachian Arts Program. Christy Farnbauch explains the type of grants made available through the program. During the Initiative, she says, there were several grants available. There was a Fast Track grant of $500 for individuals, and like the ORBI grant, it could be used for self-improvement and to help promote the artist's work, but not to help produce it. There was a mini grant of $1,000 for organizations. The review process was informal. Once a month Donna Sue, Michael Maloney, Barbara Bayless and Michael London got together, read the applications, and decided what individuals or programs to fund.

When Appalachian Arts changed from an Initiative to a Program, the mini grant was increased to $2,000, but the process was a little more formal with specific application dates and a review in-house at the Ohio Arts Council. There are two review cycles with a turnaround of about six to eight weeks.

Here are three of the stories of people and organizations who, through the arts, have made an impact in their communities with some funding help from the Ohio Appalachian Arts Program:

The Athens Photographic Project

Helen Keller said, "The best and most beautiful things in the world cannot be seen or even touched. They must be felt with the heart." Helen may have had a lot in common with the participants of the Athens Photographic Project. Like her, they too struggled to create under a perceived handicap: they were in recovery from severe mental illness. But through the help of a dedicated tutor, they let their hearts be their eyes as they learned to view an often terrifying world and select and capture a single image that represented their understanding of it.

Elise Sanford is the director of this unique project. Born in Iowa, she holds a BA in journalism form Tulane University, and a BFA and MA in photography from Ohio University. She came to Athens with her husband forty years ago, not nearly long enough to be thought a native she says. She had been doing some photography to support her journalism and thought if she had more training, it might help her get a job. She started to school at Ohio U as a part-time student in 1982. When she graduated in 1988, she was fifty-nine years old.

Elise's husband died six years ago, and his death forced her to deal, alone, with a severe family problem. "A nightmare," is the way she describes it. Their thirty-five-year-old son, under treatment for schizophrenia, was living at home at the time. He had been hospitalized for seven years but had been released. She admits that she didn't know how to deal with the situation. She saw huge gaps in services for the mentally ill. It was crisis-driven, treating people in hospitals from meltdown to meltdown or as outpatients for short terms until they were stabilized. Nothing was offered in the way of programs that would increase their self-confidence or self-esteem.

"With my own son," Elise says, "I've wondered so many times, 'How does he view the world? What does the world look like to him? Wouldn't it be wonderful to capture that?' " Trained as a visual artist, Elise set out to develop a program that would do just that.

She had a bold idea for a program that would take a group of adults with varying types of mental illness, give them point-and-shoot cameras, train them to use them, and let them capture the images in their world the way they saw them. Her son had been in a group home setting, so she presented the idea there, and the group bought into it. She immediately began hitting up her friends for funding.

Elise's reputation as a professional photographer gave credibility to her efforts. She has more than sixty exhibitions to her credit, and her work is part of many private collections. That pilot program was very successful, and Elise realized she had to continue with the effort. "We had a track record to build on," she says. "And at that point, I think, I met Donna Sue."

Donna Sue remembers meeting Elise that first time. "She was referred to me by one of the board members who had spoken to Michael Maloney. I was instructed to get in touch with Elise to discuss funding opportunities."

"For us it was wonderful to have Donna Sue as a contact person," Elise says. She was a breath of fresh air. I had tried to get funding for the project before, and I hadn't gotten anywhere. I couldn't make it fit, but Donna Sue had a way."

Elise was adamant from the beginning of her project that she did not view it as an activity but a true expression of artistic beings, and she taught her student with that same attitude. She was familiar with the Ohio Arts Council from receiving an Individual Artist Fellowship for her photography, and she wanted the agency to think of this project in the same professional way. "So we were able to get a grant – a $2,000 grant that nowhere near covers the cost, but even though it doesn't, it's very important to establish our viability as an arts program. I started from the very beginning to make sure we were looked at by other artists as professional and to get recognition for that."

Recognition came in an exhibition of the students' work in Athens called "I Have A Voice: Photographic Images by the Severely Mentally Ill." It represents the professional effort of twenty-five students. After being locally exhibited, the work became a traveling display, touring throughout the state.

Elise says her program provides the students with a safe climate and asks them to express themselves through art, while recovering their voices, which have been lost in the illness.

"It's not easy," Elise says. "I see people start in one corner of the room and isolate themselves the first time, and they slowly come over and join the group. We ask all of the existential questions: Who am I? How do I fit in? Where do I fit in? Do I even want to fit it? I can equate to that."

Self Portrait by Paul Reininga, Athens Photographic Project.
From the Collection "I Have A Voice."

Window by Jean Morris, Athens Photographic Project.
From the Collection "Our Voices / Our Worlds"

Working with the mentally ill students during a ten-week course, Elise has some insightful observations. "They are an amazing group. They are usually quite creative, quite bright, and they are very good at putting combinations together."

A strong indicator of the success of the Athens Photographic Project in helping the mentally ill students reclaim their self-esteem comes from a quotation from one of the early students: " I felt challenged to go places and deal with people that I would normally avoid. Now, instead of walking with my head down, I keep looking up so I don't miss the perfect shot," the woman said.

A core group of eight students from that first group wanted to continue their development as photographers, so Elise added two manual camera classes along with instruction in film processing and black-and-white printing. The result of that additional training is another exhibit entitled "Our Voices / Our Worlds" produced in partnership with the Kennedy Museum of Art at Ohio University in Athens.

Besides the Ohio Appalachian Arts Program, other funding from several sources, most notably the National Alliance for the Mentally Ill (NAMI), continues to help support the Athens Photographic Project. In 2004, NAMI Ohio produced a calendar featuring the work of Elise's students.

Elise, who is now in her mid-seventies, says "I've had the idea for a long time that there ought to be programs such as this. I happen to be a photographer, but it can be any of the creative arts. It can be creative writing; it can be poetry; it can be theater, music, dance. All of these speak to a group like this."

The Athens Photographic Project is a strong demonstration of the ability of art to change people's lives.

The Adams County Quilt Barns

"A musician must make music, an artist must paint, a poet must write if he is to be ultimately at peace with himself. What one can be, one must be." These are the feelings of psychologist, Abraham Maslow. He might have added to the list, "and a quilter must quilt." Anyone who knows a quilter would agree that, like other artists, they are driven to create and happiest when they are actively engaged in their art.

Donna Sue Groves has spent many hours with a woman who fits this description: her mother, Maxine Groves, a master quilter. Donna Sue wanted to find a way to honor the talent of artists like her mother and to promote their Appalachian heritage and culture in Adams County. The idea she came up with was to paint one of the designs that make up a quilt square on the side of a barn in the same way Mail Pouch Tobacco advertises its product. She presented her idea to a community-based committee of visual artists, quilters, business and property owners. Why stop at one square? they wondered. After all, twenty squares could make up a quilt sampler and, scattered throughout the county, the squares would literally form a trail that tourists could follow, admiring the artistic display while seeing something of the countryside and communities. The Ohio Appalachian Arts Program agreed to provide seed money to get the project started, and the committee began working with Planning Adams County's Tomorrow (PACT) to bring the idea to reality.

In 2001, local artists Mark Lewis and William Brown painted the first barn, featuring a ten-square-foot quilt pattern of traditional triangles and squares. The last barn was completed in the summer of 2004. In addition to the original twenty squares, several barn owners have designed and painted their own quilt patterns. And, of course, each time a new quilt barn is "unveiled" it presents an opportunity for a community gathering and a celebration with Appalachian music, food, and crafts.

Donna Sue is proud of what's been accomplished in Adams County and the fact that the project has grown beyond her original vision. "I'm just the messenger for the project," she says, "but it's such a simplistic, grass-roots, entry-level opportunity for a project and program in a county."

Other organizations have taken up her vision. Quilts are now on barns in three counties (Adams, Brown, and Monroe) in Southern Ohio, and Donna Sue envisions a necklace of quilts stretching throughout all twenty-nine counties of Appalachian Ohio.

The vision grows larger yet. In July of 2004, representatives from Southern Ohio, Eastern Kentucky, and East Tennessee met to discuss a project called "The Clothesline of Quilts in Appalachia." The project will bring residents of these three regions together to execute a cooperative vision that will preserve and showcase Appalachian heritage in a public venue.

While the Adams County sampler project helped promote pride and tourism and was an example other counties could emulate, it also tied directly to a group of unlikely artists and helped liberate their talents by offering them the opportunity to work as professionals on a mainstream commission. The Athens Photographic Project joined the Quilt Barn Project to the benefit of both groups.

Donna Sue says that she had wanted to document the quilt barns but was also being hounded by other counties, states, and the news media for photographs. She had an idea that she hoped that Elise Sanford's photographers would buy into. Did Elise think it was possible, Donna Sue wondered, for the photographers to come to Adams County to photograph the quilt barns? Elise talked to her group and the answer came back. "Yes, yes, yes."

After the logistics were taken care of, three vans, filled with eleven photographers and all their equipment, traveled 150 miles from Athens to Adams County, prepared for three days of work.

The Double LeMoyne Star Quilt Design on Goodseed Farm Barn,
5228 Old Route 32, Peebles, Ohio. Artist, Charles Reed.
(Photograph by Jerry Lindsey)

Donna Sue says. "The group was excited from the start; the trepidation didn't show until they stepped out of the vans, but once we broke bread together, they were all right."

Besides photographing the quilt barns, the group also wanted to give back something to Donna Sue for involving them in the project. They ended up photographing twenty-five of Maxine Groves' quilts. That meant unfolding them, hanging and shooting them, taking them down, and refolding them. Not a quick and easy job.

Donna Sue says, "In my life experiences of thirty years of working in community, that is my shining star, sharing that time with the group and Elise and her assistant, Jackie."

One hundred rolls of exposed film and three days later, Donna Sue had the professional photographs she wanted, and the Athens Photographic Project had the satisfaction of working as professionals and a good start on another exhibit.

The Markay Cultural Arts Center

The fiction writer, playwright, and humanitarian William Saroyan said, "The role of art is to make a world which can be inhabited." Since her organization took on the restoration of a 1930s art deco movie theater in downtown Jackson, Barbara Summers, Executive Director of the Southern Hills Arts Council, knows how difficult a task that can be. When her organization began the project, the theater was an abandoned building that was in bad shape. Drains in the roof had been plugged creating a condition that caused part of the roof to collapse, and there was standing water in the basement.

Major funding for the first stage of restoration came from the Ohio Legislature, the Governor's Office of Appalachia, Downtown Revitalization, and the Ohio Arts Council. As terrible as the condition of the building was, Barbara is proud to say that they were able to open the lobby of the theater as an art gallery nine months after her organization took charge. The Markay Cultural Arts Center had a home. "I think it's fascinating here because ten years ago, we would not have had a prayer of restoring this building and establishing a gallery, but we've just chipped away at it long enough, and now we do, and the Appalachian Arts Program is part of that."

Like many arts organizations in Appalachian Ohio, the Southern Hills Arts Council is strapped, struggling for dollars and for staff as they try to develop programs. "The Appalachian Arts Program gives us an opportunity to communicate with each other that we didn't have before," Barbara says. "I can pick up the phone and call Donna Sue and say, 'I need help;' I need help finding judges or something else. Until the Appalachian Arts Program, I didn't have that. Sometimes we live and work in isolation, and we're used to doing what we can with what we've got. That's the problem in Appalachia. It's different now. Donna Sue is so alert to what's going on. Something that's happening four counties away might impact what I'm trying to do, but I have no way of knowing that, but she does and tells me who to call about it."

The gallery of the Markay Cultural Arts Center is home not only to art exhibits but also to a variety of other arts activities such as poetry readings and knitting classes. An exhibit of the quilt barn photographs from the Athens Photographic Project was featured thanks to grant money from the Ohio Arts Council. The gallery can be rented out for private parties and events as well.

The restoration of the theater is a desire by the community to preserve its cultural heritage by returning this beautiful old building to the condition of its Depression Era beginning. The goal, of course, is to renovate the theater so that it can be used for live performances. That effort is well underway with the installation of new floors, ceilings and walls with attention paid to replicating the fibers and woods used in the original. Modern dressing rooms have been built beneath the stage with effort now being concentrated on the technical support areas such as sound and lighting.

Live performance is dear to Barbara's heart. Her background is in the theater, and she was trained as a stage manager. She is from New York and worked in theater there before moving to Jackson thirty years ago. "This is where I needed to be," she says. "I did not need to be in Manhattan. I'm a small town girl really."

As much as Barbara appreciates living in a small community, she is frustrated as well. "People here don't have a clue about their relationship with the arts. The word 'arts' frightens them. Too high tone might be it. We have a lot of trouble getting people to walk into the gallery. That's why I like to put art on the street. They will stop and look at that there.

"Part of our mission here is to help broaden the appreciation of the arts and the practice of the arts," she says. "They have a huge tradition of the arts here. Just look at all the things that are traditional. The Appalachian music is as strong as it gets; the Welsh men can't stop singing. Fiddle playing , guitar playing, banjo playing. They're all here. And, of course, quilting, knitting. All of the needle arts. But they don't recognize that. They probably think the arts are only ballet and opera and Shakespeare."

Barbara knows her organization is no longer without assistance in this area. "Part of our job is to make the arts less threatening. It's been a real battle for us here, and again, that's where the Ohio Art Council has been a big help in terms of understanding that the Appalachian region is different from the rest of Ohio."

Another of Barbara's frustrations is with the local school system. She feels that schools are not supporters of the arts, which makes her job that much more difficult. She thinks once the theater is operating, it will make an ideal location to bring students, and she can provide an additional opportunity for learning. The theater is in possession of six bas-reliefs that had been originally installed in 1940.

These figures represent different aspects of life in the Jackson area during that period. There are representations of the founders, railroads, coal miners, apple orchards, and a woman in a garden. The bas-reliefs are being restored and will be remounted in the theater. These and other aspect of the historic theater can be a history lesson in the culture of the '30s and '40s not only for the children but for the entire population.

These three examples of the value of funding for different programs of Appalachian culture are representative of the many more that exist. They have all played a role in preserving Appalachian culture and heritage through support of the arts in the region.

Christy Farnbauch thinks that by staying active and alive in Appalachian Ohio, the agency has provided a great service to the residents. "We validated work that they had been doing for a very long time, and even if they hadn't received funding from us, we still said to them that it was valuable. We also delivered on our promises. We said, 'We'll be back,' and we came back. And all the time, we made sure we had representatives who were from the region working in the region. The Ohio Arts Council wasn't like a lot of agencies that came in and were gone tomorrow."

"What is art but a way of seeing."

Thomas Berger, Novelist

18

Looking Back /
Looking Forward

It's been over ten years (July 1, 1994) since the Ohio Appalachian Arts Initiative began its goal of serving the underserved in the state. From the beginning, the Initiative and the Program that followed were a building process, a joint effort with the people and the organizations to take the strong base in the arts that already existed and to lift it up, to build a frame around it that would provide a visible structure in the area for the residents to see and enjoy and feel proud that they were part of this wonderful thing called Appalachian Arts. And if the structure was tall enough and beautiful enough, people in other parts of the state and across the nation could see it as well and know that they had overlooked the wonder of the region. Although there is still — and will always be — work to be done, those involved in helping to build this structure of Appalachian Arts can look back and take pride in their accomplishments.

Wayne Lawson: "I think it's been tremendously successful. Not just because we've found a way to put money back into the area, but because of the networking, the communication, the understanding of the importance of the arts to small communities and rural areas. The development of tourism. You can go down the list. There are about twenty-five reasons I think it's been successful. And it works!"

Michael Maloney: "Part of what the Appalachian Arts Program did was to articulate the identity of the region. We're not building something that is artificial. The most important thing is seeing the changes that have taken place in the community. What we found was a region in which the number one complaint from the most perceptive people was, 'We don't feel good about ourselves here, and our kids don't feel good about themselves, and when they grow up, they leave, and that's why this is a depressed region economically and in a lot of other ways.' So, there has been a renaissance in the celebration of Appalachian culture in Southeastern Ohio, and the Ohio Arts Council has had an important part in that."

Beverly Warfield: "I was hoping we could develop something that would last. Not something that would start up, last a couple of years, and die. I am delighted that it still exists, and that the Ohio Arts Council has embraced it. I've been able to see that it's ongoing, and people feel good about it, and that it's had a very positive impact on their communities and their organizations. It just makes my heart warm to know that it is still viable and still valuable."

Michael London: "I'm probably as skilled as anyone I know at letting go. If it's not working, I move right on. This was a project that was, for me, from the beginning, a joy. I didn't ever have to worry about how do I get out of this. Michael and I worked through long meetings and long hours, but it was not hard. It was a joy because of the people that we were working with and the kind of institutional support that was provided. It was a joy because of the people in the field that we got to meet, that we got to work with. It was a joy to be able to see that a government agency could make change within itself as well as effect change in the community. It was nice to be able to do a job and then get out of the way and watch the joy that existed in the community."

Donna Sue Groves: "This program is all about the quality of life. Not only our quality of life but also the quality of life of the people we work with. And that joy factor Michael talks about, we've all felt it. I feel the best when I've been working in a community for a while and they have worked hard on something and are successful. I feel like a mother, knowing they'll be fine. You blow them kisses and wish them well."

Caroline Pierson: "Helping people understand just how important their communities are, what beautiful and wonderful things they have around them, and how they can encourage those things to continue and mature is a powerful thing. This program has been an important link in that respect through the connections in the arts that have been formed and continue to grow stronger."

The effect of the Ohio Appalachian Arts Program on communities and organizations has been profound. Linda Basye, Executive Director of the Pike County Travel and Visitor's Bureau and Past President of Ohio's Appalachian Country, offers her thanks: "I've gotten grants from them for the arts show that we do. We got grants as awards for artists, because a lot of them didn't have the money to buy the materials to do their work. It's grown and grown every year, and you wouldn't believe the quality of the art. The artists are selling their work, so we've been able to teach them to value their work. I can't say enough about the Appalachian Arts Program. It's wonderful."

Granted that the Ohio Arts Council has met its objectives during the past ten years, and the Appalachian region has benefited, what happens to the program now? Where does it go from here?

Lakin Cook, former Director of the West Virginia Commission on the Arts, reflects on the value of ORBI: "It's probably exceeded my expectations in that I was shocked to find out it's ten years old. I think part of its success is very straightforward. It's pretty nuts and bolts, but at the same time it does what it needs to do. I also think in some ways it helps us identify trends that we need to pay attention to, from the arts community and from the local communities as they change. I think that art and community art are very cyclical."

Donna Sue knows that for the Ohio Appalachian Arts Program some things will change. "As soon as we grow up, no longer will we have two extra grant opportunities a year above and beyond the rest of the state. We are special and unique, and we can certainly say thank you for this extra grant opportunity, but we are not getting that because someone is being benevolent. They (OAC) are giving us a hand, not a handout."

Wayne Lawson wants to make sure the helping hand continues to be stretched in the direction of

Appalachian Ohio as a commitment by the Ohio Arts Council to the region. "I'm sure five years from now the program will still be going. I think it's a matter of always making sure the program is on the table the same time everything else is. Make sure there's always somebody there in the area."

The Ohio Arts Council, through the leadership of its staff and dedicated consultants, has demonstrated that the arts are as important in the Appalachian region of the state as any other. It has a continuing commitment to making the arts accessible to everyone because of the demonstrated ability of the arts to change lives and enrich the individuals and communities.

Richard Ressmeyer, Director of Arts for West Virginia, a partner in the Ohio River Border Initiative, says it best: "The arts are not a phenomenon of affluence; the arts are not a phenomenon of economic circumstances. To some extent, the arts are not a phenomenon of formal education. The arts are a phenomenon of the human spirit, and that distribution is greater than money; it's greater than political power, and that's why we're in the business."

You get a sense of the human spirit that Richard describes by spending time in the communities, visiting with the people. Travel the thin black lines meandering away from the Interstate and state highways that connect small town to village to more small towns. Secondary roads they are called. In Ohio, and in particular the twenty-nine eastern and southern counties that constitute the Appalachian part of the state, the roads link poverty with pride, regional deprivation with neighborliness and a sense of humor.

Throughout the region, one finds the self-reliance of the people, some of whom don't live "down home" anymore but have moved to larger cities (Cincinnati, Dayton, Columbus) in search of opportunity. Appalachia is people that hang on dearly to the roots of home, allowing themselves to feel the connection gently tugging on them, pulling them back to the small farms and coal mining towns, the hollows and streams, the communities that will always be home.

State Route 32, the Appalachian Highway, leads east and west through seven Appalachian counties in southern Ohio. You'll find the Amish with their beautiful furniture, crafts, and baked goods living along this route just as they do in the eastern Appalachian counties. You don't have to look very hard either to find unique names leading off to interesting locations: Tater Ridge Road, Lick Skillet Road, Burnt Cabin Road, Suck Run Road. These are names to spice up any writer's piece on Appalachia. And those roads can be found along a few short miles in Adams County. Others abound throughout the region. If Appalachian locations and its people are unique, so then is the art they create, since any art is a reflection of the beliefs and attitudes of the people who create it. Art is individual values at its core.

Art and beauty are everywhere in Appalachian Ohio. One need only look at the world through an artist's eye. Belmont County poet, James Wright sees a sewer pipe spilling into the Ohio River and finds there a beauty to inspire a poem that describes his view of the Appalachian region where he lived.

Beautiful Ohio

Those old Winnebago men
Knew what they were singing.
All summer long and all alone,
I had found a way
To sit on a railroad tie
Above the sewer main.
It spilled a shining waterfall out of a pipe
Somebody had gouged through the slanted earth.
Sixteen thousand and five hundred more or less people
In Martins Ferry, my home, my native country,
Quickened the river
With the speed of light.
And the light caught there
The solid speed of their lives
In the instant of that waterfall.
I know what we call it
Most of the time.
But I have my own song for it,
And sometimes, even today,
I call it beauty.

Beauty has always been in the eye of the beholder, and those with the talent to communicate that beauty to the inhabitants of the world around them, make life more interesting and enriching. The great opera singer, Beverly Sills, said during an NBC-TV performance in 1985, "Art is the signature of civilizations." In Appalachian Ohio, thanks to the Ohio Arts Council, that signature is written bold and clear.

Afterword

What I have recorded in these previous pages is a snapshot, a long moment in history of the years that gave birth and nourishment to the Ohio Appalachian Arts Program. Looking into my rearview mirror, I realize that the landscape has already changed. The picture no longer looks the same.

After long and valuable service, Barbara Bayless has retired from the Ohio Arts Council. Her role in starting the Minority Arts Program and, through working with visionary and selfless consultants to build the framework for incorporating and supporting an Appalachian Arts Program, is key to the success of this endeavor. She deserves the gratitude of all those who reap the benefits of the program today.

Christy Farnbaugh, whose effort as Director of Community Development at the Ohio Arts Council included responsibility for the Ohio Appalachian Arts Program has left OAC for a position in education. While missing the excitement and satisfaction of working in the arts, she is enjoying a schedule more agreeable to the mother of young children, one that allows more involvement and influence in the education of her two sons. Her contributions to the success and future direction of the Ohio Appalachian Arts Program cannot be underestimated.

Reorganization at OAC assures that the program will continue to get the attention and funding it needs. At least for now. Arts programming in an ever-shrinking federal and state budget climate continues to be an uphill battle.

The one constant in the reorganization is Donna Sue Groves, the hard-working, friendly face that Ohio Appalachian artists and organizations depend on. She continues as coordinator of OAAP, and as such, is the knowledgeable and willing advocate the region needs.

As for this writer, the snapshot of the Ohio Appalachian Arts Program that I was able to develop during the time I worked on this project hangs in a place of honor in my memory. More than anything, it helped me get in touch with my own roots — if not the actual roots, at least those that reside within and are at the core of my being. Jim Wayne Miller, the Appalachian poet I have come to admire, could have been describing me in his work, DOWN HOME: "He kept meeting feelings like / old schoolmates, faces whose names he'd / forgot. He came on feelings he could / enter again only as a stranger might / a house he'd once lived in."

My growing-up house was in the southern hills that run along the Mexican border in Arizona. I am the son of a copper-miner father and a tobacco-farmer mother from Kentucky. Those plain-talking, hard-working, salt-of-the-earth people I met in Appalachian Ohio and West Virginia wore the same faces I recognized in my own kin, fiercely proud of the little they had because they knew it had come to them honestly through their own sweat.

Jim Wayne Miller holds up another memory to me in his poem, SHAPES: "When he saw people flow-ing out of the mountains, / leaving like a line of clanking coalcars, / his life grew damp and heavy in his flesh, / turned dark and cold / as charred wood in a rained-out fire."

I remember the dreary aftermath of the mining company closing down the copper shafts and taking everything of value with them when they left my hometown, including the company store and newspaper. People like my folks were left wondering rightfully what had happened to the value of their property? Who would buy a home in a ghost town? Those same questions resonated through the near-abandoned coal towns I drove through in southern Ohio and West Virginia.

But Miller's poetry and the wonderful experiences that fueled me during my time working on this project also lead me to embrace more positive things that influenced my writing: I was reminded that people still worked for ideals. That with commitment, part-time jobs had nothing to do with the hours you worked, only with the money you got paid. When I saw daily how important the creation and sharing of art was to people and their communities, how much they were willing to give of themselves in the process, I could not help but treat the writing of the history of the Ohio Appalachian Arts Program with the same respect. In doing so, I did my best to live up to the title of this piece by celebrating, honoring, and valuing the rich tradition of the arts in Appalachia.

Wayne Rapp
Summer 2005

About the Author

Wayne Rapp is a freelance writer whose nonfiction has appeared in such publications as *Ohio Connections, Stone in America, Slippery Rock Gazette, The Columbus Dispatch, The Catholic Times,* and *AirFare.* One of his pieces, "Lessons from Underground," is part of the Bottom Dog Press collection *Writing Work: Writers on Working Class Writing.*

His fiction has appeared in a variety of publications, including *Grit, Thema, The Americas Review, Vincent Brothers Review,* the *Bottom Dog Press Anthology, Working Hard for the Money,* and the Fall Creek Press series, *VeriTales.* His short story, "In the Time of Marvel and Confusion," published by *High Plains Literary Review,* was nominated for the Pushcart Prize. He has completed a collection of Border Stories called *Burnt Sienna,* and his fiction has twice been honored with Individual Artist Fellowships from the Ohio Arts Council.

Attributions

- Jim Wayne Miller, "Abandoned," "Turn Your Radio On," "Down Home," "Shapes" from *The Mountains Have Come Closer*. © 1980 by Jim Wayne Miller and reprinted by permission of the Jim Wayne Miller Estate, literary executor, Mary Ellen Miller.
- James Wright, "Beautiful Ohio" and excerpt from "The Old WPA Swimming Pool in Martins Ferry, Ohio" from ABOVE THE RIVER: THE COMPLETE POEMS by James Wright, introduction by Donald Hall. © 1990 by Anne Wright, introduction © 1990 by Donald Hall. Reprinted by permission of Farrar, Straus and Giroux, LLC.
- Donna Sue Groves, "Appalachia!" published by permission of the author.
- The mural "Protecting Our Children" published by permission of the Pomerene Center for the Arts.
- James Wright, "Autumn Begins in Martins Ferry, Ohio" from *The Branch Will Not Break*. © 1963 by James Wright and reprinted by permission of Wesleyan University Press.
- Danny Fulks, "The Way We Laughed" from *Tragedy on Greasy Ridge: true stories from Appalachian Ohio*. © 2003 by Danny Fulks. Excerpt reprinted by permission of the author.
- Self Portrait by Paul Reininga from *I Have A Voice*. © 2001 by The Athens Photographic Project. Reprinted by permission.
- Window by Jean Morris from *Our Voices / Our Worlds*. © 2002 by The Athens Photographic Project. Reprinted by permission.
- The Quilt Barn Project Photographic Team by Effie Mullins. © 2003 by The Athens Photographic Project. Reprinted by permission.
- LeMoyne Star painted by Charles Reed and photographed by Jerry Lindsey. © 2003 by The Athens Photographic Project. Reprinted by permission.